TIME OF MY LIFE

TIME OF MY LIFE

Myf Warhurst

hachette
AUSTRALIA

hachette
AUSTRALIA

Published in Australia and New Zealand in 2022
by Hachette Australia
(an imprint of Hachette Australia Pty Limited)
Gadigal Country, Level 17, 207 Kent Street, Sydney, NSW 2000
www.hachette.com.au

Hachette Australia acknowledges and pays our respects to the past, present and future Traditional Owners and Custodians of Country throughout Australia and recognises the continuation of cultural, spiritual and educational practices of Aboriginal and Torres Strait Islander peoples. Our head office is located on the lands of the Gadigal people of the Eora Nation.

A catalogue record for this work is available from the National Library of Australia

ISBN: 978 0 7336 4918 9 (paperback)

Cover and internal design elements by Christabella Designs
Cover photography by Cameron Grayson
Typeset in Scala Pro by Kirby Jones
Printed and bound in Australia by McPherson's Printing Group

The paper this book is printed on is certified against the Forest Stewardship Council® Standards. McPherson's Printing Group holds FSC® chain of custody certification SA-COC-005379. FSC® promotes environmentally responsible, socially beneficial and economically viable management of the world's forests.

To my family, who have always encouraged me to live differently x

Contents

Introduction

*'Music ... can name the unnameable and
communicate the unknowable.'*
Leonard Bernstein

That Mr Bernstein is one clever fella. Of course, we knew that already because of the incredible music he wrote. But he also nails in one short sentence the reason music is so important. It connects us, consoles us, lifts us up and helps us make sense of our place in the world. It can also make us think about where we want to be in the future.

Music and lyrics have almost always done that for me: named the unnameable and communicated the unknowable. They have taught me a great deal and been a constant my whole life. My love of music would help define my career.

So, it can't be that surprising that, in sharing stories from my life and lessons I've learnt along the way, music would be the narrative thread that stitched them together.

Like so many Australian kids growing up in a rural community, being a long way from the big smoke meant TV and radio were things that helped me feel connected. The bands I loved and the music I listened to made me feel not so distant. And when I left home and started living in the not so mythical big smoke, music helped me find 'my people'. Some of those friendships are still going strong.

In telling my story I hope I spark some memories for you, give you some laughs and maybe even something to think about. But, most of all, I hope it makes you remember the music, the bands and the lyrics that mean the world to you. And that, in remembering, you get to re-live all the great moments, all the profound moments and all the sad, joyous and defining moments that make up your life.

I have re-lived times that are embarrassing, lovely and perhaps shouldn't be shared. Keanu, Beyoncé, Daryl Braithwaite, Sting, Dolly Parton, Kenny Rogers, Olivia Newton-John ... okay, now I am just namedropping to get your attention.

Like you, I have more to do and definitely more songs to hear, but I can honestly say, up to this point, I have had the time of my life!

– Myf

Howzat

(Garth Porter and
Anthony Mitchell)

1.

We are family

There are pivotal times in every life and for me nearly every one of those has a soundtrack. I have chosen to open this book with a family memory. You know them, the stories that are woven into every gathering, every celebration dinner and then repeated over and over so that in the end you aren't sure if the memory is yours or has just been absorbed into your brain so you think it is. Most of the Warhurst family memories have been retold so often that I suspect the original tale is so embellished that the fine line between fact and fiction is forever blurred. In our family, if a story has given everyone a few laughs, it becomes entrenched in family folklore. But even with collective memories, what we home in on and how we choose to remember can be very different and personal things.

The fact that this particular memory involved a satin-clad, shirtless male pop star, with an enviable 1970s-style mullet hairstyle and a twinkle in his eye, who went on to sing Australia's unofficial anthem, makes this tale even better, and it is one I'm happy to embrace as wholly my own. Mostly because it illustrates exactly who I was at the time and gave strong clues as to who I was to become.

It's Sunday night. I'm around three years old. I've got long, blonde hair (I know, you're shocked as I'm now as dark on my noggin as the mission brown paint my dad loved to coat everything with in the '70s, because it was going cheap). My fringe is cut thick, chunky and a little off-kilter thanks to my mum's, shall we say, enthusiastic, home hairdressing skills.

I'm wearing denim overalls and a stripey skivvy combo that I think would look absolutely on trend now. Clutched in my chubby, grubby hands is my special blanket. Most kids have something they latch on to for security and simply can't live without. Mine is a scraggly, cream-coloured, barely holding together wool carcass of a blanket with a satin edge. I call this blanket my Nap Nap. When I sucked my thumb I'd simultaneously rub that rancid blanket on my nose in a comforting manner. Standard, revolting three-year-old stuff.

I am the youngest of four kids (I have three older brothers), and when this oft-remembered incident famously took place, we lived in a 1960s small cream brick veneer house in the country town of Donald, about 240 kilometres from Melbourne, in central Victoria, in a street where, if you looked past the row of houses on the opposite side, there was nothing but wheat fields as far as the eye could see. Wheat was the main economy of the town, as was the abattoir on the edge of town. There was a horseracing track, a pool, a football field, a local newspaper and a main street with three pubs that were built in a time when the promise of finding gold brought people and money to the area. Both had long ago deserted the place.

It's Sunday night. Australia's favourite pop music TV show *Countdown* is on the tellie. Every Sunday me and my three brothers would gather around the Rank Arena TV in the corner of the living area for our weekly communion. This show was our church, where new pop songs from around the world were revealed to us like sparkly offerings, and we kneeled at the altar with an almost religious fervour. What this means is, we all sat glued in front of our black-and-white TV, hoovering up the content like our lives depended on it.

Out of all the revelatory moments that Molly Meldrum and *Countdown* delivered, there was one song that changed everything for me. I think you'll know it. Everyone in Australia who grew up in the '70s would have heard it.

It starts with a loping bassline that steps up and down in a rhythmic fashion; slow, creeping, slightly urgent, also ominous. Something good or bad (or a little bit sexy, not that I really knew what sexy was back then) is clearly about to happen. Basslines had that power in the '70s. Ba dum, ba dum, ba dum, ba dum. Then the male vocal begins telling us he believed the lies the subject spun and that he was the one.

Verse two confirms the deceit of the subject of the song (no prizes for guessing the subject in question has been fooling around), and then the chorus starts. A trio of voices build like a musical round, each voice adding a new layer of urgency and a tiny hint of '70s prog rock frippery. '*How ... How ... Howzat!*'

My brothers might have looked cool and unmoved, but my mind was blown. I was feeling things that I'd never felt before. What was this song? Who were these men on my screen, in *my house*, combining two of my favourite things: cricket and music? This was even better than when I was stuck at home with the mumps and allowed to drink flat lemonade. Treats like that were pretty rare in our house.

My love of cricket can be attributed to the fact that I lived in a house full of boys and I loved everything they loved. Mum had played hockey for Australia and Victoria, my dad was apparently a gun at local footy and cricket, and my brothers all excelled at whatever sport they turned their minds to. Me, on the other hand, didn't show too much promise in this department. But regardless, I adored what they adored and this is also probably why I also watched *Countdown* religiously at such a young age. They loved it, so I did too.

This family love of sport led to watching a lot of sport on TV, but I worked out later that watching Test cricket was about as interesting as watching question time in parliament, and you could be guaranteed that nothing ever happened until you left the room to go to the toilet. I reckon the popularity of Test cricket back then was due to the fact it allowed the menfolk to zone out into a state of mindfulness (shutting out the world, sitting still, emptying your mind, and doing nothing, for hours on end), at a time when mindfulness would have been laughed at, along with the concept of sheilas getting a mortgage in their own names or not having to give up working when they were pregnant, or other such unbelievable societal progressions.

So back to the huddle of Warhurst kids in the lounge room on that particular Sunday night ... here's this song about cricket, I was instantly in, but it seemed odd that these men were wearing decidedly un-cricket-like clothing. Their attire looked neither functional nor comfy. It looked positively stifling in certain areas. There'd be no way you could bend down to retrieve a ball in silly mid-off in those trouser boa constrictors. The singer caught my eye. He was wearing a velvet and satin jacket with lapels so pointed and wide that they could probably take an eye out or, even better, rudder a small boat. The jacket, was, of course, worn with no shirt underneath (it was the '70s, nipples were everywhere), and was paired with a pair of light-coloured satin pants that creased ever so suggestively where the top of the legs met the torso, leaving little to the imagination about the choice that one singer had made when he got dressed in the morning. We've all heard how satin is unforgiving, but in this case, *that* was clearly the point. These were the type of going-out clothes that maybe a young, hot new teacher from the city might wear to a dinner party where my mum would impress the guests, serving up beef bourguignon for dinner (it's French, don't you know?), matched superbly with a sweet riesling direct from a Coolabah cask, and finished off with those posh chocolate After Dinner Mints that came in individual brown wrappers. So sophisticated.

I placed the song in the camp of adult stuff, with cricket leanings. I was utterly entranced.

I continued to watch, and felt something stirring within me, something that would connect me to that little brown box with moving pictures in the corner, and the sounds that emanated from it, for the rest of my life.

Deep from my brown vinyl beanbag, which squeaked with every move, I arose. My chubby limbs seemingly driven by an unknown force. I walked zombie-like towards the tellie, knowing full well that Mum was about to yell at me not to get too close because I'd ruin my eyes. I didn't care. I was being led towards a bloke named Daryl by a force so strong that I was ready to sign up to whatever satin-and-velvet-clad cult he was leading. I stood directly in front of the television, placed my hands on the screen, felt that initial buzzy electric pulse that only a valve TV screen can give off, then pressed my face on the screen and proceeded to pucker up, giving Daryl Braithwaite, resplendent in his daring satin pants, a big ol' sloppy kiss.

But it wasn't just Daryl that I had fallen for, it was everything that he represented. The storytelling through words and sound, the fashion, the lights and drama, the music, the intrigue of a glamorous world out there with strange, bewitching things beyond my small town. Somewhere so exciting that people wrote songs about what happened there so everyone could hear about it. I wanted to be part of it.

I should acknowledge that Daryl did not consent to the kiss I planted on his face, nor was he ever aware that this happened and so, for the record, I apologise in writing here for my objectification of an unknowing gentleman in satin pants. It was very clear though that, at that moment,

I had messed about, Sherbet had caught me out, and I was a goner.

From that time on, music, and my love of it, became my obsession. Put simply, Daryl Braithwaite from Sherbet was my gateway drug (and I bet you never thought that sentence would ever be uttered).

About thirty years later, I was able to tell Daryl this story, when he came on the ABCTV music quiz show *Spicks and Specks*, and I could tell he was genuinely chuffed. Or slightly embarrassed. I'm not entirely sure which, really. Either way, despite my cool demeanour, I can guarantee that little Myf was squealing on the inside.

Daryl not only had an effect on people in the '70s, he managed to back it up again in the early '90s, this time by singing a song that has since become one of Australia's unofficial anthems, his version of the Rickie Lee Jones' song 'The Horses'. This slick, adult contemporary ditty chock-full of '80s tropical island keyboard is now adored across generations, from older folk like me, who lived and loved through it the first time while we wore high-waisted pleated chinos matched with boat shoes and a grandpa shirt, thinking that we looked just like we'd stepped off a yacht, to millennial AFL footballers who sing the song in their clubrooms after winning a game. Why this particular song has captured the imagination of so many disparate types is inexplicable. Even Daryl himself has said that he can't put his finger on why it's an ongoing success across generations.

None of us know what that song is really about either. The lyrics are obtuse: telling a little darlin' that we'll go horse-riding. It's a song with such a broad musical palette, it lets the listener place their own meaning into the words, and therein lies the appeal. 'The Horses' is vague enough that it can be about whatever the hell you want. And that, my friends, is what music is all about. It offers us mere mortals a way to access feelings and make sense of our thoughts, at times when we might not have the emotional or intellectual language to do so on our own.

The first time I heard 'Howzat' I didn't have that language but I knew enough to know those musical moments meant something special. They changed me. And for that, I am truly grateful. Thanks Daryl.

Dancing Queen

(Benny Andersson, Björn Ulvaeus
and Stig Anderson)

2.

Dance like nobody's watching

B esides my *Countdown* epiphany, it was Mum and Dad's parties that I remember best from the Donald era of my early life. Those, and watching *The Muppets* on my birthday for the first time in colour on our brand-new colour TV (a momentous occasion in the Warhurst household). Otherwise, it's really all a bit of a blur. Days and nights followed the usual weekly patterns. I was regularly pinned down by any one of my brothers, who would perform a game called 'The Typewriter', where they would pretend to annoyingly type on me and then roll the fake paper roller by twisting my ears. If I was lucky, they would finish by dribbling on my face, saying they were just applying the liquid paper required to cover a mistake.

This game, and farting on my head at any opportunity, were big faves in my house (well, my brothers' faves, I was not as enamoured of the experience). I idolised my brothers and put up with the ear twists because I loved hanging around with them. This was my role as the (sometimes annoying) little sister. When they got sick of me, they'd tell me to go to my room and draw a horse. Which I would do, happily, for hours. I perfected how to draw a horse but that early artistic promise never sparked so I am afraid that is the extent of my visual arts career.

Mum says it was so hard to get me to go to bed as a kid, let alone sleep at night, because I was worried about missing out on something exciting. Apparently I was quite the howler. These days I still have the same arguments about going to bed every night, except I have them with myself. Even though I'm nudging fifty and know that I desperately need my eight hours a night so my face doesn't look like I've been run over by a hair crimper, I still drag my feet about going to bed. There's something in me that continues to believe the most interesting things happen in those dark hours of the night. They never do, of course. The old adage, 'Nothing good happens after one am' is true. Pity I don't ever listen to myself.

But in our house at Donald sometimes good things did happen after bedtime. Mum and Dad were both art teachers and the reason we had moved to Donald, from Portland in regional Victoria where I was born, was because Dad had been offered a position as the headmaster at Donald High School. Being sociable folk, Mum and Dad were keen to get to know the locals after we moved, so they held dinner parties and staff gatherings at our little house, which would go late into the night. I clearly remember being put to bed many times, furious that I was missing out on the action, but strangely comforted by the sweet aroma of cigar and cigarette smoke wafting from under my closed bedroom door.

Smoking indoors was perfectly normal in those days. Many years later, I took a boyfriend to stay at Mum and Dad's house, and Mum, knowing that my boyfriend smoked, offered him an ashtray so he could smoke inside while we had a glass of wine. I nearly fell off my chair. I hadn't been part of that culture since share house life in the '90s, where we all thought we were so cool because we sat next to our own ashtrays, puffing away while watching *Beverly Hills, 90210* on TV. Dylan McKay was still a spunk even through a smoke haze!

Dad is an artist and plays piano by ear and Mum is a fabulous seamstress, artist and potter, so when they rolled into town with us four kids, they brought with them a love of teaching, Gilbert and Sullivan musicals and old-time melodrama theatre productions. It didn't take them long to spread that love. They would put on these huge shows once or twice a year and the whole town would get involved. It was brilliant. This was a formative time for all of us kids, as each of us discovered a love of the stage at this time. I attempted to follow in Dad's footsteps to become a great pianist (obviously, I didn't ever get to the Richard Clayderman heights I so clearly aspired to in the '80s, though I have photos somewhere of me sporting a hairstyle like Clayderman's glorious, feathered mullet). Two of my brothers, Kit and Andre, would both follow their musical passions by playing in their own bands. My eldest brother, Shaun, gave theatre a go for a while, too. Thanks to our parents, we all have a love of performance. I imagine it's lodged somewhere on the back shelf, deep in our DNA.

After the closing night of a show's hugely successful run, where everyone in the town would attend (there was literally nothing else on so it was the highlight of Donald and its surrounds' social calendar) there would be the after parties. Of course we kids got to go, but our appearance was limited to a quick hello, and if we were lucky the older kids might steal a sip of alcohol from an abandoned glass and then, already dressed in our PJs, we'd be sent off to sleep in what was then known as the 'Mobile Babysitter', the family car. Look, what can I say? It was a simpler time.

The parties Mum and Dad held at our place were my favourite. I'd spend much of the night looking through the frosted glass sliding doors, ubiquitous in those '6os joints, facing into the 'good room', which was located at the front of the house. The good room is a relic of times past. Back then, it was the only part of the home where children weren't welcome to hang out, because it was full of the 'good furniture' that was saved for use when guests came over. As a child, I thought this unfair. Why couldn't I go in there and play with the trinkets on display with my greasy, Teddy-Bear-biscuit-covered fingers?

I totally get the concept of a good room now, even though the idea has fallen by the wayside. It was a practical idea, really. The rest of the house could look like the aftermath of a Keith Richards' hotel room party (and with four kids I imagine ours did most of the time), but if a guest came over unannounced, you could simply pull the sliding doors across and, tickety-boo, the guests could recline in the plush velour of the on-trend burnt orange, velvet couch, without them seeing the hallmark grubby hand marks and food crumbs that come with having young children.

I remember peering through the frosted glass into the good room and it was filled with the coolest people I'd ever seen, aside from those on *Countdown*. They looked so different from the people we'd see in the main street or at the grocer. It was like they had all morphed into different beings. Shiny, happy people. They were eating a spread of '70s delicacies – square cut cheese and cabana speared together on toothpicks, celery sticks filled with cream cheese, and Mum's favourite party favour: white bread (crusts cut off), containing mayonnaise and soggy tinned asparagus, rolled up and held like a little piggy in a blanket with another of those ubiquitous toothpicks. *Ooh la la.* (Side note: I have to admit I have craved this asparagus treat ever since I wrote this line. Once you get over the fact that asparagus from a tin has a rather slimy mouth-feel, it's quite the culinary revelation. You should try it some time.)

I thought everything adult was posh and sophisticated when I was a kid. When Mum pulled out the big guns to serve real coffee from the percolated coffee machine, you knew the guests were *very* important. Most of the time Mum and Dad, and every other adult I knew, drank Nescafé Blend 43; there was none of this takeaway coffee business back then. If you can't instantly remember the stale breath of a teacher who's sunk too many cups of Nescafé, chased with a Winfield Blue cigarette, did you even go to school in Australia in the '70s and '80s? I think not.

At the end of proceedings, Mum would roll out the After Dinner Mints. I would collect the small paper bags they came in the next day and sniff them, imagining a future where I too could serve such a sophisticated chocolate to my guests.

The signifiers of affluence, or at least the understanding of the signifiers, were much easier for people to access back then. These days the signifiers are an Insta-worthy jet-set lifestyle or an architect-designed home, but back then it was pretty simple: if you had a double-storey house and a pool, then you were obviously millionaires. If you took a family holiday to Queensland, you were way out of our league, and if, like our neighbours in Donald, you had a speedboat named *Alebrad*, which was their two children's names combined – Aleta and Brad – then you were certified royalty.

We might not have had the pool or the speedboat, but we had a record player. To us, it was the most valuable thing in our house. It sat in the corner of the good room, and I was told *never* to touch it. It was far too expensive and precious. Only my oldest two brothers, Shaun and Andre, were allowed to use it without Mum and Dad in the room. Kit and I hadn't really mastered the art of properly dressing ourselves at this point, so it was probs for the best we weren't allowed to even touch it.

But, in the same way I was drawn to the satin majesty of Daryl Braithwaite, I was of course inexplicably drawn to fiddling with the record player. I'd seen Mum put on her copy of Neil Diamond's *Hot August Night* on a Saturday morning a million times, while she did the vacuuming. I'm pretty sure every household had a copy of this record in the '70s. What was going on with that weird cover photo of Neil in his bedazzled double denim Canadian tuxedo playing what looks to be an air saxophone? I've never quite understood that choice but I was obviously the minority. Whoever sat down with him and said, 'Neil, this is a great pic that captures everything about this one hot night in August,' was a marketing genius. It sold a gazillion copies.

Occasionally Mum would also play another '60s and '70s staple, Bert Kaempfert's *A Swingin' Safari*. This one featured a classic '60s-looking gal on the front wearing a sexy short safari suit, topped by a pith helmet that barely contained her bouffant hairstyle, alongside some culturally inappropriate artefacts to signify that Bert had been to Africa once. To me, this girl looked like a classier version of the women I'd seen on *The Benny Hill Show*, who would run around rather fast, sometimes without tops on, to the soundtrack of Boots Randolph's 'Yakety Sax'. You know the one. No one blinked an eye when it came on the tellie in prime time. This was all very normal.

Not surprisingly, most record covers from this time featured a woman on the front in a suggestive outfit of some sort, usually for no reason at all. My all-time favourite of the 'album cover showing an underdressed female for no obvious reason' was the Australian music compilation series that went under the name *Ripper*. Each year of '75, '76 and '77 had an image of a woman's arse in a ripped pair of shorts, with the artists' names on the exposed butt cheek. What's not to love about an unphotoshopped pimply bum advertising that Fox's 'S-S-S-Single Bed' song (which, incidentally, I thought was about a very innocent sleepover – I guess that's correct, sorta?) is inside? I was sold!

But one day I'd had enough of simply looking at the record covers, I was determined to master that record player. I'd watched Shaun put a record on, probably something by AC/DC, and it didn't look that complicated. It was as simple as putting a black circular thing that makes the sound on a round thing with a stick in the middle. Then all you had to do was pull a lever downwards and a stick would move of its own accord across the round thing and drop onto the edge. Hearing the pre-crackle before the music started let you know you'd done it correctly. Sweet.

While Shaun's AC/DC records terrified me – they were far too dark for my young ears – I was obsessed with a record that I suspect most Australian houses had alongside their copy of *Hot August Night*. It was Abba's *Arrival*. This was another record cover that I fixated on. I was entranced by the matching white jumpsuits of the four very attractive young Swedes in the photo, they were all just so perfect. This, combined with the sweet pop magic and the tinge of melancholy that they created with songs like 'Dancing Queen', 'Knowing Me Knowing You' and 'Fernando', had me spellbound. I pored over that cover as if it was the *Encyclopaedia Britannica*, which again, only rich people had.

It was as if Abba had arrived by spaceship (or by a futuristic helicopter at least) into our small house in a tiny country town with only wheat fields beyond the last row of houses. I don't think I'd ever seen a helicopter before, let alone matching crotch-splitting jumpsuits such as these. It was all packaged in a fold-out cover, which meant I could look at more pictures of these incredibly glamorous creatures *again* on the inside. Beam me up, Scotty.

The moment inevitably arrived when, driven again by an innate desire, I crept into the good room and went straight to the record player. I gingerly took the record out of the cover, slid it out of its plastic sleeve, and placed it on the turntable, then pulled the lever, which was quite a feat for my uncoordinated fingers. Success! The much-anticipated crackling sound started, followed by the sweet, sweet sad sounds of a band whose music is now imprinted in a million histories worldwide. Little was I to know at the time that the event that spurred those four musicians towards fame was a European song contest called Eurovision and, years later, I would have the job of hosting the live Eurovision broadcasts for Australian viewers. Young Myf would never have believed such magnificence would come her way.

But before all that, there I was, in the forbidden environs of the good room, in my own fantasy world, dancing alone to Abba. For that moment, I *was* the Dancing Queen. At least I thought I was alone. In actual fact, the whole family was watching and laughing at me through the frosted glass sliding door. It was so amusing to them that I didn't even get in trouble.

Again, I was learning that music allowed me to tap into a portal that helped me express a yearning inside, before I even had the language to express it. And that was the urge to not only dance like no one's watching, but to wear a white jumpsuit like those perfect Swedish babes. Sadly, I only managed to implement one of these things into my lifestyle as I grew up. White jumpsuits are simply too unforgiving.

Y.M.C.A.

(Jacques Morali, Victor Willis and
Henri Belolo)

3.

Long live disco

In those early Donald years, Mum and Dad came up with a brilliant idea that would set our family on a trajectory that made us a little different from most. I suspect it came about because having four kids meant money was tight. So my parents worked out a way to make a bit of extra cash and, at the same time, retain a connection with Dad's family, who were all based near Mildura in the area of Sunraysia, right at the tippy-top corner of Victoria. The area is known for its grape and citrus produce. When Uncle Rob, who lived in a place called Darling View, on the mighty Baaka, the Darling River, about twenty kilometres out of the New South Wales town of Wentworth, told Mum and Dad about a sixty-acre property near his going for practically nothing, they snapped it up. The land had orange and mandarin trees and the goal was that our family would pick the fruit from those trees during school holidays.

Aside from where the earth met the water and life was fecund, everywhere else at Darling View was covered in scrubby bush and salt flats. It was mostly a dry, desert environment. Anything that grew or lived there survived against the odds. There is a harsh beauty to this difficult landscape that speaks to me still.

Darling View was on the way to a little outback town called Pooncarie, where our grandfather Abe, who we called Pop, was living at the time. Pop didn't suffer fools or any kind of bullshit (his favourite word) from anyone, especially children. We kids knew our place and trod carefully around him. Pop was once married to our nan, who had been a glamorous singer back in the day. Pop went off to the Second World War as a gunner, miraculously came back (not many gunners did, apparently), they had a few more kids, then they separated. Nan remained in the family home and we saw her quite regularly given she lived in Irymple, which was in the area. The rest of Pop's life was quite a mystery to me. From whispers I found out he was an SP bookie in South Australia for a time, but when Mum and Dad bought the land at Darling View he was living in a converted bus. Pop loved the river and the bush, and when we travelled with him it was in a battered Mini Moke, sans walls and roof, and of course no seatbelts.

He wasn't the most cheerful bloke and the only time I saw Pop truly happy was when he was relaxing in his bus after a day's work on the land. From what I can gather, Pop was a bit of a nomad. He spent much of his life travelling around the desert areas shooting rabbits, and living off the money he made from selling their skins. In the bus, I witnessed him at his happiest, playing an ornate 1970s organ. You can see them in the back of op shops now. They're the ones with dual keyboards and loads of coloured buttons promising a samba or marimba drumbeat, with many foot pedals to control the basslines and sound.

Pop's life, like Nanna's, was very hard. Relying on the land to survive was not an easy prospect in those days. There wasn't a lot of time or room for laughter or fun. I suspect Pop carried some trauma from the war too, but none of that was discussed in those days. Pop didn't talk about feelings. Maybe the music did that for him. I just know that when I was there watching this old, weathered man happily churning out a few tunes on an organ in his bus, in outback Australia, it was pretty joyous.

I imagine this is where my own dad got his extraordinary talent for piano, too. Pop and my dad were very different in so many ways but their love of music was a bond they shared. Neither of them was taught how to play, they both simply played what they heard. That's quite a skill.

My dad still plays piano, and, like Pop, he seems happiest when he is embellishing a trill at the end of a song and lurching into the next crowd-pleaser. It must be genetic because there's nothing more hilarious than our family gathered around the piano at Christmas, all rosy from being a few sherbets deep, while Dad rips out a cracking version of 'Can't Help Falling in Love' and we all sing along, badly. That's a Warhurst Christmas, right there.

I suspect Mum and Dad's next project on our new property was inspired by Pop's bus, or perhaps it had its genesis from an article that Mum saw about an artist's retreat in a converted tram. She tore that story out of a magazine and kept it in her special drawer in her bedroom. That same drawer housed her bottle of 4711 Eau de Cologne, which was the perfume *du jour* of the '70s, even though I vaguely remember it smelling like peppery antiseptic cleaner.

My parents had a vision. Instead of us all sleeping either in the shed or our burnt orange VW campervan when we stayed up at 'the block', the dream was that we should find something a little more permanent, and a little less lived in and loved by the local snakes and rodents. Not having to share a dwelling with snakes is enough motivation for anyone to rip pages out of a magazine.

This is one of those moments I am pleased I don't remember, but one night Mum says she saw a huge black snake on the dirt floor where our camp beds were. Then it disappeared. There was a fruitless search and then the horror of us all going to bed knowing that a clear and present danger was still possibly in the vicinity and could quite likely slither back looking for mice or rats or us for its dinner. I don't remember if I slept well that night but Mum didn't. In the morning, the search resumed to find the snake. No one thought about the welfare of the poor creature in those days – the snake catcher was simply called a shovel. 'Kill the bastards,' was Pop's oft-said refrain.

Now that I am writing this, I do remember the next day clearly, because we were forced to spend the entire time in the above-ground Clark pool that Dad had just purchased and hastily set up next to the shed. Above-ground pools in those days weren't quite like pools today, they were essentially just a blue plastic tarp and a bit of rolled tin that made the wall, all held together by clamps and plastic. On recalling these pools, the exposed raw tin of the walls seems particularly unsafe for children to be around. Never mind. We filled ours using the hose from the water tank. No chlorine or filters for this baby. Just brown water direct from the Darling River.

Our cousins had a proper indoor inground pool, surrounded by PebbleCrete, which we all thought was extremely exciting and quite the step up from our Clark pool. Everyone (including me) also thought it hilarious when Uncle Brent would put the powder chlorine into the pool and get me to swim around in it to mix it into the pool by calling it 'grow', promising that these chemicals would give me a growth spurt, which, being a short arse, was something I desperately wanted to have. Sadly, the growth spurt never really happened, and now that we know what's in chlorine, it might have actually been the reason why it did not. It was a different time.

Summers at Darling View were so hot – most days were usually over 40 degrees – so for a kid who loved water, being forced to stay in the pool for as long as it took my parents to find the snake was just *the best*. At one point the snake was finally spotted but slithered up into our parked car, where it promptly disappeared into the interior engine mechanisms, never to be seen alive again. A few days later a terrible smell emanated from the car and confirmed our suspicions that our snake friend had found its tomb in the car's motor. There was no such thing as air conditioning for us, so winding down the windows was enough to blow the smell away and allow us to drive the car (and for Mum to sleep soundly) again.

The snake incident might have sped up Mum and Dad's plans a little. In the late '70s Melbourne City Council was clearing out some council items from its storage facilities, which included their gorgeous old green W Class trams.

These trams were the ones that used to rattle up and down the streets of Melbourne from the earliest of days. Some still run on the tourist routes today. They were going for the measly sum of five hundred bucks so Mum and Dad purchased one. The idea was that it would be converted to live in, with bedrooms at the ends and a kitchen in the middle. Kind of like a caravan, I guess, but weirder – a bit like our family. I can't imagine what the locals must have thought when our W Class tram number 477 arrived, some 600 kilometres from Melbourne, on the back of a truck. It was then lifted by crane onto a besser brick foundation. I suspect that many people in the district hadn't seen a tram in the flesh before then, let alone travelled on one. I hadn't.

The arrival of the tram remains one of the greatest of our family's collective memories. That, and the fact that after selling the block our family built a mud-brick house (my brothers built the bricks, while I mixed the mud, too young to do much else), designed by renowned Eltham mud-brick architect Alistair Knox. That experience, of living differently, had a huge impact on my adult life. Since then I've always taken a keen interest in architecture. I understand the satisfaction and pride that can come from living differently, knowing that architecture can be a deep expression of who we are. To outsiders, our family was a little bit weird, and did things differently. This was especially obvious as we were living in a part of the world where no one had even heard about mud-brick houses, let alone thought it possible to live in one. But we were proud of this difference and proud of what we had made. No amount of fitting in will ever replace that feeling of creating something that was ours.

I adored our family life in the tram during the holidays. I got to share a room with all of my brothers and we formed a happy but extremely naughty gang. And when I was bored with them I would take myself off to the driver's compartment at the front and pretend I was a driver for hours on end. Ding ding! Who needs Thomas the Tank Engine when you've got your own tram?

In the kids' section of the tram, which was down one end (Mum and Dad had the other end, with the kitchen in the middle), there were four beds, jammed head to tail. Elsewhere, there was only room for a tiny black-and-white TV that barely got reception unless we pulled the aerial around all the time. When it was working we watched the cricket, *Countdown* and *The Muppets*, and Mum and Dad watched the ABC news. The tram had an evaporative air conditioner that we used in summer when the temperatures were unbearable. I'm not sure who thought regularly pouring a bucket of water into an electrical appliance that was *on* was a safe thing to do, but I am genuinely amazed that no one died using it. I sometimes think families had more kids back then because there was a chance that you might lose one or two along the way. There were no safety regulations on anything! 'Here, kids, have some plastic bags to play with.' What a great idea! They may as well have said, 'Pop them on your heads and seal them so you can blow them up to where you can't breathe. Now isn't that fun!' So many things we did as kids are just unheard of now. Breathing in second-hand smoke was the norm and seatbelts were a luxury.

With the tram safely ensconced on our block of land, we became Blockies. Properties in Sunraysia were known as blocks because that's how the land was originally dished out to returned servicemen after the First World War: in blocks. It was part of a government scheme where returned servicemen were leased land to grow fruit on or house livestock, which, given the climatic conditions, would have been near impossible for most people who had no experience in that neck of the woods. Hindsight tells us that this program was also established to get men who may well be damaged after the war out of the cities. Understandably, many didn't go the distance on their properties, but the name 'block' remained. If you come to Sunraysia and you even attempt a saunter through a block with a glass of cheeky Pinot in your hand like you're in a vineyard in the South of France, you'll be laughed out of town. No one lived or worked on a vineyard, it was a block; and no one was a farmer, you were a Blockie. End of.

So there we were, on our block, every winter, spring, summer and autumn holidays. My older brothers had to work the land with Mum and Dad but I was considered too young to pick fruit or weeds. I got the good end of that stick. I would disappear for an entire day on my own, wandering the adjacent sheep station, Kelso, or scouring through rubbish piles that were dotted randomly through the area. On the riverbank, I had found some pieces of a broken Willow pattern plate and I was determined to find all the pieces to show the tragic story of the star-crossed lovers and make it whole. I never did find them, but I didn't stop trying for a long time. I was clearly easily entertained (or slightly obsessed – I will leave you to decide).

I also got to live out my horsey girl fantasy that most young girls dabble in at some time or other. Dad's other brother, Uncle Neil, as well as being a Blockie himself, bred horses, and, always the opportunist, he saw our block as the perfect new space for some of his horses to graze on.

Uncle Neil had a very specific dream of breeding a perfect Appaloosa. Apparently, the reason for this was that Appaloosas were Elvis's favourite horses, and Neil, who was also musical like Dad, played the saxophone. No surprises that Neil's favourite sax player was Boots

Randolph – he of 'Yakety Sax' Benny Hill fame – who was also Elvis's saxophonist. I loved Uncle Neil and listening to him play sax might explain why I feel a connection to Elvis deep in my bones.

So, thanks to Uncle Neil, I had a horse at the block. My horse was a grey Welsh Mountain pony named Tom Thumb whose main skill was avoiding being ridden by never being caught, as well as throwing off anyone if he got a whiff they were just the slightest bit nervous. He was, as Uncle Neil would say, 'a bloody bastard'. I once made my brother Kit get on Tom Thumb, knowing full well that my horse had a shifty habit of puffing out his stomach when you tied up the saddle, and when riding commenced he would then suck his stomach in and the saddle would slip underneath, ensuring the rider fell off. Tom Thumb was never one to disappoint so, after convincing Kit to get on (he hated horses), the saddle inevitably slipped and Kit slid off into a massive prickle bush. I was elated. All those years of the typewriter torture were instantly avenged. Kit still talks about the horror of the prickles to this day. And he continues to not ride horses.

When I got Tom Thumb, Uncle Neil lent me a Western saddle. It was a beautifully crafted piece of leatherwork, like the ones you'd see in old Western movies, with a big pommel on the front for the rope that you might need to lasso a calf. I thought I was the coolest cowgirl in the world.

My leanings towards things that were a little bit country started with that saddle. It was a fast ride from Western saddle to fully fledged country music fan, aided by the fact that the only music you could hear on the radio in Darling View was the local ABC radio station and a local commercial station that played pretty much country music all day, every day, unless it was broadcasting a syndicated replay of American Casey Kasem's legendary Top 40 show. I listened to that religiously late at night on a small tape player that also had an AM radio dial.

Whenever we drove in our uncle's car, or worked with any of the local fruit pickers, the soundtrack was country music. My love of singers like Glen Campbell, Dolly Parton, Patsy Cline, Kenny Rogers and Charley Pride comes from this time. Country songs are simple things, full of drama and heartbreak, of loneliness and bad behaviour, all taking place in less than three minutes. In country songs, life was hard and lonely, something I keenly felt in the haunting Jimmy Webb song made famous by Glen Campbell, 'Wichita Lineman'. When I heard that song about a man who worked on the phone powerlines, hoping to find the voice of his love somewhere in the middle of nowhere, a connection, I felt that deeply. At the block I was a long way from anywhere, wanting to find a sign that I too could connect with the outside world, whether it be through completing pieces of blue pattern on a plate, through a radio transistor or through pop stars. The outside world was still otherworldly, untouchable. But when I listened to certain songs, I felt a little more connected to something much bigger than the world I knew.

It wasn't just Warhursts on that block. A couple, Laurie and Shirl, also lived there. They lived rent free, entrusted as caretakers if anything needed sorting when we weren't there. Laurie worked for Uncle Rob, picking fruit, doing maintenance, and Shirl was his partner. When everyone else would go out working on the block, if I wasn't hunting for broken plates I was visiting Shirl. She'd make pikelets for me, dripping in margarine (margarine was considered the healthy option in those days, before we realised it was basically melted plastic). A smoke was never not dangling from Shirl's mouth, and a longneck bottle of beer was always open near to hand. There was also an entire room in their house that was full of empty bottles and rubbish that had built up over time.

I didn't really comprehend what was going on, but I knew that something was not quite right in their world. Laurie and Shirl fought a lot, which we could hear from the tram, and one night we heard Laurie threatening to shoot Shirl with his gun (everyone had shotguns out there, something I find hard to fathom today). There were no phone lines to call the police. That was the night I learnt that there was another, more sinister side to this isolated rural way of life. The world there was very tough and many folk had ended up on a block because there was nowhere else for them to go. I learnt later that Laurie had done time in gaol. Breaking the cycle of poverty and alcoholism can be too tough in the best of times, but near impossible when you're so far from anywhere.

At night, we kids would sit out staring up at the stars while waiting for Mum to heat up my favourite treat of a can of Tom Piper Vegetables and Sausages (clearly, I have expensive taste) in an aluminium pot on the stove.

In the daytime, the best days were when I would ride on the back of the boys' motorbike through the bush. They had a little grey Honda XR 78. We'd do circle work in the muddy salt flats, and Mum would be furious when we returned because the backs of our clothes would be covered in mud, kicked up by the back tyre. Good times.

The other highlight of our days at Darling View was swimming in the dangerous Darling River. This river mostly had sandbanks, so immediately from the river's edge the bottom would drop to great depths. In order for me to be able to swim in the river, a rope was tied around my waist, under my arms, and attached to a stake in the ground on the bank. If I was to encounter any trouble, or disappear for too long underwater, Mum could just yank me back up by the rope! Easy! Sure, Child Services would probably be called today if such a thing was witnessed, but for us this was completely normal. Mum has said recently that it wasn't a rope that was tied around my waist, rather it was a car tyre, but I suspect that maybe she hoped that was the case.

I also remember learning how to use an air rifle (a 'sluggy' we called it) to shoot at cans and trees. Sluggies didn't use bullets, they used little weird metal balls that apparently can't kill you, but they could definitely maim. No worries then on the day Shaun accidentally shot Andre in the back of the leg with the slug gun, and the surprising thing is that we all laughed about it, like it was perfectly normal behaviour. Like I said, things were different back then.

On Mum's birthday one year instead of some jewellery or a nice handbag, Dad bought Mum what we called Mum's Snake Gun. 'Happy birthday, Nancye, please enjoy your special day with a gun to kill snakes.' At least it was better than a vacuum cleaner!

You might have guessed by now that I got into trouble a lot up at the block, mostly for doing the naughty things the boys did. The most trouble I got in was when I released some half-dead rabbits (they had been shot but weren't quite dead) from a wheat bag that was sitting in the back of Uncle Rob's ute. I was an animal lover and I couldn't understand why everyone was so angry at me for doing what I thought was the right thing. I hadn't learnt that there was little time for kindness and emotion in the bush. Or that those cute little Peter Rabbits, that looked like they appeared straight out of the Beatrix Potter picture book I was reading at the time, were up to the gills with myxomatosis and were destined to die painfully, regardless of my freedom-fighter actions.

Life was very different up in the bush, and usually far harsher than I wanted it to be. Most nights, as the temperature soared over forty, I sat within centimetres of the air conditioner that was battling to make a difference in the relentless heat, whingeing about having a headache, Dad would say to me, 'You'll never be a pioneer woman.' He was absolutely right. And I didn't want to be. I didn't want to deal with the harsher realities of life, and death. Finding pieces of a broken plate to piece together while listening to country music and thinking I was going to be a cowgirl was more my jam. (Yes, I know, a true cowgirl's life is right in the middle of those harsh realities but I was only young so we'll just have to let that slide.)

Strangely, it was during the later years up on the block that I pushed country music aside and discovered disco. Sure, I had seen some disco songs on *Countdown*, but when Uncle Rob and Aunty Maureen decided to take us all to the movies in the big smoke of Mildura to watch my first-ever film on the big screen, it was the Village People's first and only foray into film, the now legendary flop, *Can't Stop the Music*. I'm pretty sure that experience set me up for wanting to hang out in discos with shirtless men dressed as uber sexy cowboys and construction workers, singing about places where young men can go when they're short on their dough, for the rest of my life. HEAVEN.

I had no idea at the time what it all meant. At such a young age I genuinely thought one of the Village People's other songs 'Milkshake' was actually about making a milkshake, rather than shaking another type of big, thick and frosty one which, according to the song, still gave you all the protein you needed at lunchtime. When I finally worked out the double entendres, my lifetime love of all things camp, kitsch and fabulous began.

Through the Village People, and too many others in the contemporary music and pop world to mention here, it became clearer to me that music was a safe place for people who felt different; artistic types could present in a knowing way, without belying their true essence. Music could be a ticket to freedom and for many, at a time when being gay was still a criminal act, they could hide in plain sight and beam their message into lounge rooms all over the world, authenticity intact. This, I realised later, was a very radical act.

I was fortunate to know nothing about the 'Disco Sucks' and 'Death To Disco' mantra of the very opposite punk movement that was happening at the same time in the '70s and '80s. Many punks hated disco, they derided it as bland music to sedate the boring masses. Their angular, aggressive punk was seen as a rebellion against everything disco represented, which on the surface was capitalist dreams of success and fun. What some punks missed entirely was that the people making disco, while gaining very mainstream success, were mostly from the margins of society – Black, Latino, LGBTQ – who originally made music for themselves, to make their own lives better. It was only because it was so good that it was co-opted by the mainstream. This disdain of a particular musical form may also have been bound in something else, too. Given that punk was a predominantly white, Western musical form, and the domain of mostly men, it is possible that there may have been an element of racism, sexism and homophobia to this attitude. Not all punks, of course – from punk there has come some extraordinary musical moments that changed the musical landscape forever and pushed the boundaries of inclusion and taste – but, for lovers of anything creative, it is an excellent lesson in the old cliché of never judging a book by its cover. When someone says that something's not cool maybe question their ingrained prejudices before you make a decision about what's important or is worthy of attention.

The explosion of disco also saw the international success of Australia's own Bee Gees – Barry, Robin and Maurice Gibb – whose terrifyingly extraordinary falsetto voices went global on the coat-tails of the disco movie *Saturday Night Fever*, which also helped cement John Travolta as a star. The brothers Gibb actually hailed from a suburb in Queensland called Redcliffe and, coincidentally, after the Donald years, my family was about to move to a town of a similar name in Victoria, called Red Cliffs. While there is absolutely no connection whatsoever between me and the Bee Gees – their dizzying heights of fame have only been matched in my life by the height of my hairstyles in the '80s – somehow I find the thought of us both knowing the joys and hardships of growing up in a small town named after red cliffs quite comforting. Back then I also had no idea that the Bee Gees would become a recurring musical motif in my future life.

Islands in the Stream

(Barry Gibb, Maurice Gibb
and Robin Gibb)

4.

Living the dream

Moving towns and schools as a kid is never much fun, no matter how outgoing you might be. In my first week at Red Cliffs Primary School, because both my brother Kit and I didn't know anyone, we had to do the unthinkable and spend lunchtime together. This pleased neither of us. It was more than enough that Kit and I shared a bunk in our bedroom in the Warhursts' new Education Department–owned house (most country towns had a house set aside for teachers to rent, so when one rolled out another rolled in to take over). Kit made it known that he thought I was his embarrassing little sister, and I hated him because when it was lights out he would flick spit on me from the upper bunk, which would hit me like delicate drops of rain in the dark. Yes, hilarious, Kit. You deserved every bit of being thrown off by Tom Thumb. I regret nothing.

These days Kit and I are best mates so there is a chance that this lunchtime experience bonded us, just a little. But the future is a different planet and the Red Cliffs–dwelling Kit and Myf weren't at that stage yet. So, it was a little grim through that first week of a new school, sitting with my brother, with nothing to say to each other as we ate our sausage rolls, drank our orange Prima and scoffed our Summer Roll bar from the tuckshop. I never understood why the tuckshop wouldn't serve regular chocolate bars, like a Mars Bar or Chokito, they had to go for the pretend-healthy alternative, which in reality was a poor cousin of the real deal and had just as much sugar. Somehow the makers of Summer Rolls (and Space Food Sticks) held a monopoly over school canteens, to the detriment of all other chocolate bars.

Sitting with Kit at lunchtime wasn't the only reason school didn't start out well. Mum made us wear school uniforms even though they weren't compulsory at Red Cliffs Primary. How to stick out like the proverbial dog's balls! During that first week, no one else was wearing a uniform except me and my brother, and I found out pretty quickly that my dress was the right colour but it was the wrong style of chequered print. I might as well have held the letter 'L' for loser with my fingers to my own forehead and pointed at myself at the same time on those first few days.

Red Cliffs wasn't a very big joint, population around 2500 people, so when our motley crew rolled into town in our burnt orange VW campervan, the type now favoured by hipsters who hashtag #vanlife on their Instagram posts as they make living in impossibly small quarters look bohemian and chic, the entire street came out for a very unsubtle country perve. It was like when busybody Mrs Mangel would peer through the curtains on *Neighbours*, but the country version was to just come outside and stand and stare. No messing about.

No one blinked an eye that the youngest child (me) was seated in the back of the van in that little area more commonly known as the boot. It wasn't enclosed, but it definitely wasn't a seat, just an area between the back seat and the rear window; a place where dogs might sit these days, separated from the rest of the car by a meshed barrier. As long as I had my special blanket, which I was still dragging around at the age of eight like a weirdo, I was fine.

We were moving to a small three-bedroom house in another prestige location on the edge of town in Kurrajong Street, Red Cliffs. This time it wasn't wheat fields as far as the eye could see, it was rows and rows of grapevines that we looked out on behind our back fence. Red Cliffs was specifically set up in the 1920s as a Soldier Settlement town, and grapes were the trade that the locals settled on to produce because they had access to irrigated water supplied by the mighty Murray River. Vines are everywhere in Red Cliffs, every second person is a Blockie, and all kids pick fruit after school in picking season. Oh, and it's called Red Cliffs because of the red cliffs on the Murray River where the town is. I'm sure you worked that out but just in case.

Dad was primed to take up a new post as the principal of the local high school and Mum was going to teach art there too. Our dog, Butchie, a wilful beagle who could never be contained in any enclosure, somehow managed to break out of our backyard and find his way to the high school a few kilometres away on Dad's first day. Butchie proceeded to waddle through the assembled school kids and teachers, and sit directly at Dad's feet, panting and smiling and wagging his tail as proud as punch that he'd found his way to the all-important action. Dad, knowing that acknowledging owning a mangy mutt with a patch of missing skin on the back of his tail from scratching himself too much on his favourite tree, and a few ugly warts, probably wasn't the best first impression he needed to give, proceeded to ask the crowd who owned such a magnificent beast and if they could please take responsibility for him. I wasn't there but even if I had been I would have said nothing too. None of us owned up to owning Butchie in public. Mostly because he would hang out in front of the one takeaway food shop in town after school waiting to catch any fallen hot chips, so to get him home you'd have to push through the hedge of cool older kids wearing skin-tight Fabergé jeans, Kayak shoes and shark-tooth necklaces, and smoking Peter Jackson cigarettes, and I was way too scared to do that. Butchie lived out his charmed life spending his days in the park with the local crew who gathered daily to drink, and he probably had more friends than most humans. One day, when Red Cliffs was beaten by Mildura in the local footy competition, Butchie arrived home for dinner spraypainted in the colours of the winning team (not Red Cliffs) and resplendent in their footy jumper. Mildura's team members had stayed in Red Cliffs to celebrate in our square and to rub their win in. Butchie was happy to oblige.

Mum told me recently that Butchie was never desexed, because that was just not a thing that you did back then, and dogs did just wander the streets at will. I hate to think of how many little versions of Butchie beagles there would have been running around town over the years. If you drive through Red Cliffs and see a lot of beagle types, I guess you have the answer. Amazingly, Butchie never got hit by a car while he was out, even though he would cross major roads on his own, daily. The irony is that when he was very old and deaf and blind, he walked out behind Mum's car as she was backing out of the driveway.

Poor old Butchie. He died doing what he loved. Which was whatever the fuck he wanted, whenever he wanted. If only we could all live like the king that Butchie was.

After a week at school, both Kit and I had made a friend or two. I was befriended doing a backflip on the monkey bars by a girl called Lucinda, who is still to this day one of my best friends. The reason she befriended me, she told me later, was because she liked my watch and my ponytails were longer than hers. Those are some heavy grade three prerequisites, but I passed.

I sat next to Lucinda on one of those small wooden desks that were so old they had a space for a quill pen and ink. There was also a compartment under the tabletop to hold rulers, pens and various essential grade three things like Hubba Bubba bubble gum, and knuckles and marbles that we'd play with at lunchtime. Having a friend made grade three much easier because, frankly, most days that year were terrifying. Our teacher, let's call him Mr James, was an angry man in his later mid-life who sucked his breath through his teeth as he walked around in his Farah slacks with his hands clasped behind his back. It seemed to me he was always ready to explode. When he did, he had an ample selection of mischievous students to choose from, and he seemed to take great pleasure in smacking them heavily on the arse with a one-metre ruler because he did this on a daily basis. Corporal punishment was still legal back then and Mr James's punishments were not unusual or even frowned upon in most schools around the country. I had come from a school where teachers wore rollneck wool skivvies and let you hold their hand and clasp onto their legs if you felt sad, like that photograph of Lady Di at the kindergarten. Mr James definitely didn't subscribe to the Lady Di school of childcare or teaching. I thought he was terrifying. He would laugh maniacally as he practised his golf swing on any poor kid who had stepped out of line and been called to the front. They'd have to bend over and then, with much theatricality, he'd thwack the recipient's butt with the intensity one would have aiming for a hole in one. I never got hauled to the front of the class for a classic thwacking but was regularly hit on my hands for holding my desk open or on the back of the neck if I was too slow to get something out of my desk or was talking too much. Which was often.

Mr James would not get away with behaviour like this today. He'd be in gaol. I often think about what kind of a person could hit a child in grade three. We must have been so, so tiny and he so, so angry. But again, it was a different time. Kids were expected to be seen and not heard and were disciplined through fear. Sadly, I reckon most of the parents probably thought he was doing the right thing, because that was what they'd experienced from their schooling and parents. When people say that kids are too soft today, I always think that the fact they aren't being beaten by a strange old man with a large ruler is a sign that we have progressed as human beings and kids will be the better for it.

It didn't take long for Lucinda and I to become firm friends and we hung out after school too. I was envious of her because her mum and dad were young and hip. I was born when Mum was thirty-five, which at the time was pretty late for a mum. And, yes, if you're thinking it, I can confirm I was a mistake! Mum told me years later. This explains the very close proximity of age between me and Kit too. But I like to think of myself as a nice mistake.

Luce's mum drove a brand-new Sigma sedan that had a red velour corduroy interior. Her dad was a builder, so their house was inevitably amazing with dark clinker brick and lots of ferns. It was all very '70s, and hip. I was particularly in love with their toilet wallpaper: black, with some sort of Art Nouveau-style design in gold. Très fricken chic. People weren't afraid to make a room to poo into a fantasy land back then. I like that sense of adventure. It's far more interesting than the white on white on whitewash of today's interior design.

Luce also had Barbie dolls. Loads of them. I couldn't wait to get to her place of an afternoon after school and start playing pretend sexy relationships between the Barbies and Ken. Interesting that we had lots of different

Barbies to choose from, and yet there was only ever one Ken. Lucky Ken. Lucky men, I guess.

I had one Barbie but I could never bring her to the table when I'd go to Luce's to play (we didn't call them play dates back then, just play) because I was ashamed of what I'd done to her. She was called a Kissing Barbie, where you pressed her back and she puckered up, and she wore a fabulous sheer pink late '70s-style maxi dress that I would wear today if it was my size. Sadly, by week two of my Barbie ownership, I'd cut off her hair to see what she looked like without it. Anyone will tell you that a Barbie with her hair cut off is more akin to a Mr Potato Head with playdough squeezed through it. Barbie's hair only came through a couple of holes in chunks so she looked more like Bride of Chucky. A harsh lesson for someone with only one other doll.

Having Lucinda as a friend opened me up to a larger friendship group, and together we navigated the ups and downs of Red Cliffs life. The big questions were asked at this time. What's better, footy or cricket? What's cooler, Ford or Holden cars? Did you watch *Countdown* or the Johnny Young talent show on Sunday night? Our house obviously fell into the *Countdown* side of the audience, and I stood staunchly by the opinion that Johnny's *Young Talent Time* wasn't cool because they didn't sing their own songs. I had three older brothers who told me that, and

I believed them. I accepted everything my brothers said, although secretly I prayed to whatever god I thought would listen that I would wake up one day and be miraculously just like Tina Arena who was the star of *Young Talent Time*. I was so in awe of her. Tiny Tina Arena was everyone's fave and I desperately wanted what she had, which was to have cute boys with big brown eyes singing love duets with me. Pre-teens singing love duets is kinda weird now, but again, it was all perfectly normal back then.

Thankfully though, if I wasn't watching *Countdown* I would not have come across one of my greatest musical loves of the time (a love that is still going strong today), country crooners Kenny Rogers and Dolly Parton. Their song 'Islands in the Stream' was a number one hit in Australia in December 1983 and it went on to become one of the highest selling singles of 1984.

I knew of Kenny from my hours of listening to country music up on the block. We also had a Kenny Rogers best-of compilation tape in the car, which got played on road trips, so I was already well versed. I also loved him because he had a beard that made him look like Santa. My reference points were pretty limited. I was ten. But this was enough.

Up until this point, I hadn't seen the likes of Dolly Parton before. She looked almost alien. Huge blonde hair, massive boobs to balance out the high bouffant hair, all atop an impossibly teeny-tiny waist. She sang with the voice of an angel but had a whip-sharp retort for every occasion and a knowing smile. She was the first to make a joke about herself and how she looked but this clearly established her as the smartest woman in the room. No one messed with Dolly. Her rhinestone outfits were garish, but as a little girl who had three brothers and only one good doll left, Dolly was like a precious ornament in a snowdome. I couldn't stop looking at her.

When Kenny and Dolly duetted on the harmony and key-change-heavy and impossibly, perfectly cheesy song 'Islands in the Stream' (written of course by the Bee Gees) it was magic. Kenny with a twinkle in his eye, and Dolly, a tacky Queen of Country with a sparkle in her eye too, singing a song where they professed their love and gave each other knowing looks. For a long time I genuinely thought they were in love and was devastated to learn later that this was all for the cameras. I hadn't worked out that acting was part of the deal in music performance.

Regardless, I was sold: hook, line and sinker. I knew then that while I would probably never be Tina Arena, with her singing talent and success, one day, maybe I could be like Dolly. Dolly made you feel like that. Like there was a chance. Of course I had no idea of her superstar status then, and I would never get close to anything Dolly has achieved, but I would later come close to Kenny, for a very, very brief moment.

You might be thinking by now that for someone who made a career out of working on the national youth radio station Triple J and then on the music quiz show *Spicks and Specks*, that most of my song choices so far aren't particularly edgy, or cool by contemporary music standards. There's a reason for this. Growing up in a small country town pre-internet meant that accessing any music outside of *Countdown* was virtually impossible. You also had to wait *aaaages* to read about your favourite pop stars in magazines, or order in something you wanted specifically from the one music shop in the area. Mum and Dad didn't have much of a contemporary record collection either. While they sang and played in musicals, collecting records just wasn't their thing.

I was developing my taste from what I could scramble together from my brothers, the radio and TV, and magazines. I was starting from nothing. I'd make compilation tapes of my favourite songs from the telly, by recording on a tape recorder I set up next to the television speaker. Such a sophisticated set-up meant many of those tapes contained not just my favourite songs, but also my voice yelling at my brothers to 'SHADDAP' as they were ruining my recordings. This is also how I know not just the music from clips like Lionel Richie's 'Hello', I memorised the dialogue too. This, I've since found, is an extremely niche skill.

These days though, I question ideas around taste. Taste is subjective and I am of the firm belief that you are free to like whatever you like, regardless of what anyone else thinks. I suffered for many years being a little embarrassed of my formative taste, because people who I believed knew better than me thought them somewhat trite, so I hid them like a secret shame. Especially during the '90s when the 'alternative' to the mainstream was picking up speed in terms of popularity. Like shedding braces in grade six then pashing boys (I never had braces, but I did pash boys), as I aged I shed my love of cheesy commercial songs, stored them away for a while, and started exploring a different kind of musical landscape, less driven perhaps by commercial success. But gradually I realised that the people who thought those songs somewhat trite were missing the point of music – that it is about what *you* think! And you can like it all, or not, but you should never shame someone for having a different musical opinion from yours. Now I am able to celebrate the simple taste of that little girl who loved to escape through sparkly pop treats. There is no such thing as a guilty pleasure. It's simply a pleasure. And we've all gotta start from something.

Also, having lived a bit now, it's easy to recognise patterns. In terms of trends – whether it be in food, fashion, music, style – everything is cyclical and comes back around in a slightly different way about once every twenty years. A bit like you might drink at an airport because it's five o'clock somewhere in the world, you can listen to whatever you like because someone will think it's cool at some point in the future or has in the past. Or not. I mean, hell, it's okay to listen to Phil Collins non-ironically these days. If I had admitted during the grunge era of my late teens that the piano ballad 'Against All Odds' was my favourite song to play on the keyboard I would have been howled out of the room.

In a perfect example of the way things come full circle, by 2012 I'd embraced my secret shame and almost got to be Dolly for a second. You wouldn't believe it. I still don't. I was making a documentary called *Nice*, exploring all my formative and early loves. In a massive coup, I managed to swindle an interview with the now late, great Kenny Rogers. Our production team travelled to Atlanta in the US to interview him.

I have to admit, seeing Kenny in the flesh was a bit of a shock. After a facelift in the early '90s, contemporary Kenny didn't quite look like the same as the 'Islands in the Stream' Kenny I'd loved for all those years. My producer, Susie Jones, made an astute observation that those who got plastic surgery in the late '80s and early '90s now look a bit like the special effects in '80s movies do today –

the work is not quite there but you get the idea. Susie is brilliant and hilarious and spot on with her observations, always. Anyways, because of this 'work', which was quite controversial at the time, because, like Jennifer Grey in *Dirty Dancing* after a nose job, he came out looking markedly different, ensuring that people questioned if it was really Kenny behind the eyes. Post facelift, I have a feeling Kenny had to ditch the beard because he couldn't grow one anymore, only a goatee, because the hair that would have made his beard would now be coming out from under his eyeballs. None of that ended up counting. It was definitely Kenny in that room with me. Warm, real and so accepting of a strange woman from the other side of the world who had loved him in the '80s and loved him still in a weird fan kind of way. I wanted to know what he thought of the whole thing, because it would help me understand a little more about why he still took up a huge amount of space in my heart and the hearts of others.

As we sat in an oddly sterile function room next to piles of stacked conference chairs at the bottom of a hotel in Atlanta, Georgia, Kenny Rogers started to sing the opening bars of 'Islands in the Stream' to me. He invited me to sing Dolly's part with him. I cried. Kenny gave me my moment to live out a dream. And for those brief minutes, I was transformed. A long time ago I had imagined a life beyond the limited opportunities available in the small country town I grew up in and here it was, writ large. I still can't explain what Kenny does to me, but he definitely had something going on.

P.S. Kenny also owned a southern fried chicken joint that was popular in the US. Sadly, the chain was originally named Kenny Rogers Chickens which, if you think about it, will make you laugh a lot. Thankfully, it was swiftly changed to Kenny Rogers Roasters, which though still a bit wrong, is not quite as funny.

Xanadu

(Jeff Lynne)

5.

Are you there, God? It's me, Myf

Most people don't forget their first record purchase. It's significant, because it's the first time that you're hellbent on getting something that is exclusively yours – no one decided you needed this, you decided you *wanted* it. No one gave it to you. You saved up the money, you went to the store to pick it out, and you took it back to your bedroom to pore over it, looking at it for hours, staring at the pictures of glamorous folk whose lives seemed a world away from yours. The first album is the first tentative step towards becoming your own person. It's a big deal, at least it was back then; these days, it's not quite as significant given the number of ways you can access music now. But vinyl is having a resurgence so maybe buying your first album will become significant again (that full circle thing I talked about!).

Music, like fashion, works as a signifier of taste, an outward projection of how you want to be seen; it's a way of telling the world who you are or who you'd like to be, and a child's first foray into expressing this is pretty much the beginning of the end for parents who are reticent about their kids growing up. It's happening. The minute a kid gets a taste of showing the world what they're into through their first record purchase, unstoppable changes are well and truly afoot. Next comes clothing rebellion and defiance over parental rules, then Mum crying because she found a half-smoked cigarette in your denim jacket top pocket and you're being dragged off to the doctor to talk about embarrassing things like contraception.

In my case, obsessed with music as I was, buying my first record happened pretty early in my life. I was around eight years old. I'd saved up my pocket money (which back then would have been all of twenty cents a week), and when I finally had enough, I went to the big smoke, which was the town of Mildura. Hardly a bustling metropolis, but it was half an hour away from Red Cliffs by bus and it had a shopping mall with a water feature, which I thought was pretty bloody fancy. There, I would peruse the aisles of the one music store in the whole region, Mellberg's Music Store. Unlike city record stores, this place had to cater for all tastes, which meant mostly country music, so when it came to popular music, the selection was pretty slim pickings.

I was obsessed with Olivia Newton-John. I don't think I'd even seen *Grease* at this stage (too grown up for me), but the gorgeous Australian blonde in the lead role of Sandy was all over the television. Let's not focus right now on the fact that the entire message of *Grease* is that you have to change who you are for the hot boy to finally love you, instead let's just focus on the brilliance that is the magnetic Olivia. She was at the prime of her life, an Australian who had become an international superstar. To me, she was everything.

Xanadu, a film about love and rollerskating (what's not to love?), was a commercial and critical flop at the time, but as I had never seen it (only the music video clips on TV – again, I was too young for the movie), I thought it must be a masterpiece. Watching it later, I realised it wasn't, but no biggie. I'd asked for some rollerskates for Christmas, and getting the *Xanadu* record was the next step to me fully evolving into an Olivia Newton-John–type figure in my mind. She was impossibly beautiful, with a singing voice that could soothe (and also terrify any cats within earshot when she sang that high note at the end of the song 'Xanadu'). In my young, unformed mind, Olivia was what the perfect woman should look like. How they should present. How I should be. Of course I looked nothing like her, and the realisation that I never would was yet to dawn, but Australian TV was extremely white bread at the time, with few women in starring roles, and those who were had a look and a body type that I hadn't quite realised would never be attainable for me (five-foot nothing and slightly round).

In the '70s and '80s not many women presented the news on TV nor worked on radio – their voices decreed not authoritative enough, apparently. Apart from Margaret Throsby, Katrina Lee and Jana Wendt, women only presented the weather. Quiz shows like *Sale of the Century* had Delvene Delaney and the models who lived in the mythical gift shop showing off possible prizes by elegantly fluttering their hands over a desirable object like a diamond-set memento from Bruce and Walsh (if you know, you know). When Alby Mangels' adventure film *World Safari* rolled into town to screen at our local civic centre, where the entire town turned up with their camp chairs to watch the film in the hall, the female sidekicks were impossibly hot blonde models in string bikinis, who mostly just decorated the place with their hotness. This was what I saw in the media. It's no wonder I looked towards music to see a much more diverse bunch of women, because they sure weren't on mainstream television. There were no women who looked like Madonna or Cyndi Lauper or

Whitney Houston reading the news. I didn't know anyone in my town who looked like these women on television, but I guess I assumed that they were what the real world was like, and that this was what I should aspire to. Elle Macpherson, before she became known as 'The Body', was the face of TAB cola – with the jingle about it being the drink for beautiful people, which was repeated so we were all clear on that. It also trumpeted that it had less than two calories in the can. And there's the kicker. People I aspired to be were not only beautiful, they were skinny.

Commenting on young girls' bodies was normalised. Grandmas, who'd put themselves through the diet pills and cabbage soup and white wine diets of the '60s and '70s (imagine the bloat, people!), would happily pull a cheek or pinch a bum and announce that we were getting a little chubby. I think many women saw it as an act of public service, to drum it into us little ones so it would save us from having to go through what they did: being judged on their weight and their appearance. It's kind of a benevolent forewarned is forearmed approach. But it set us up for a lifetime of unhealthy focus on the inadequacy of our own bodies. Body shame holds back too many women from doing something bold.

My understanding of what was deemed attractive seeped into my consciousness very early, and I worked out quickly that I wasn't it.

The early warning signs were there. I wrote a note to my mum pleading to get my ears pierced and my reasoning was utterly bizarre. I started with emotional manipulation and then flat-out demands (the brazenness of pre-teen Myf is rather impressive), but the real reason I wanted the earrings was plain and simple. I didn't want to be left out and I wanted something to help me look attractive. Because I didn't think I was. And that's what I thought mattered.

Dear Mum,
I'm not quite sure how to say this, but I won't be able
to wait until I've finished school to get my ears pierced.
I couldn't bear it. All my friends will have them
done and I'll be the odd one out. My face isn't very
wonderful, so I do need something to brighten up my
face a little.

That is just the beginning. Flicking through the diary I wrote when I was eleven, in the month of August there's a page simply called DIET (caps lock Kanye style, ahead of my time, I tells ya).

I must lose weight before the swimming season.
OK so now I'm going to lose weight I have to get rid
of all that FLAB.

DIET
Breakfast – Nothing
Lunch – Egg and lettuce sandwich
Tea [that's dinner for non-country folk] *– a*
SMALL amount of what's given to me.

The manifesto goes on:

I'll have to try to stick with these rules and try not
to eat in between meals or after school. No more
chocolates or stuff like that. Each day I'll write down
each thing that I ate that was wrong and hopefully the
list will slowly disappear.

Another fun fact about this diary entry is that it came from a book called *The Judy Blume Diary*: 'Start on any day and use it all year', 'The place to put your own feelings'. I guess in the '80s this was an early version of the journal, but journalling wasn't really a thing yet. And I wasn't very good at writing in it either. There are only about four entries. One about a boy, two about a diet, and one about how much I hated my mum for not letting me go to the local blue light disco.

It seems appropriate that I put these explosive teen feelings in a Judy Blume book though, because Judy was deemed to be the queen of young adult fiction in the

'70s and '80s. Since we had no internet, just libraries, and we lived for any hint of salacious text fuelled by the smell of the printed word, Judy Blume books were like gold bullions. The one copy of any of her books in the school library was borrowed so quickly that when you did get your hands on it, it went straight to the school oval where we would sit in a circle and collectively read passages out as if it were a sacred religious text. I'm pretty sure I learnt all about periods from Judy Blume's *Are You There, God? It's Me, Margaret.* I lived in fear of getting my period because of the description of those ancient, cumbersome, humungous sanitary pads described in the book and religiously did the arm exercises outlined in it that were meant to make your boobs bigger, chanting the mantra, 'I must, I must increase my bust.'

Judy's follow-up, *Tiger Eyes*, was another page-turner; beyond grim (teenage girls love a dark tale, don't they?) but it also had a rather sexy and mysterious relationship with a stranger embedded in it, and that meant it too got read aloud in hushed tones on the oval while we all pretended to be cool and acted like we weren't really listening to the sexy bits, but were also really paying attention to the sexy bits.

Anyways, back to the diet.

1st day of my diet

*My diet went ok today. I had no breakfast. I had a small
iced coffee for lunch which I must have otherwise I'll get
too hungry. Had nothing after school. Went for a run,
felt great. I must do it again for the rest of the holidays.
I got hot and had an icy pole and a couple of peanuts.
For tea I had half a tin of soup and a piece of toast.*

I've then written, *I could have gone without the icy pole and
peanuts.*

Clearly, I'm so confused at this age because I want to look
like the girls I see on TV and yet I've got no idea what food
does and how important for growth and development eating
the right food is. Yes, it was a different time, and we know
so much more today, but it's messed up. And if I was doing
this to a small extent, many other girls were too. Secretly
monitoring our intake, restricting our choices, eating less.

Good to see, though, that I refused to drop the small
Big M iced coffee on day one of my diet. Probably because
I was also obsessed with the Big M girls, who were used
to sell Big M flavoured milk by wearing string bikinis,
looking extremely hot and accidentally missing their
mouths and instead pouring the creamy liquid down
between their boobs in a provocative manner. Advertising
in the '80s was wild, wasn't it?

New Year's Eve 1985 held the promise of the actor Gil Tucker from the Australian TV show *Cop Shop* hosting a NYE gig on the Mildura footy oval backed up by the Big M girls (doing exactly what, I'm not sure), and I was determined to be front row. It was a highlight of my life to this point when I volunteered to go up on stage to sing Peter Allen's 'I Still Call Australia Home' in order to win a copy of *Breakdance*, the video, while the Big M girls watched on in their flavour-coloured bikinis. Sure, our house didn't even own a video machine to play that videotape, but that was beside the point. I wanted it all so bad.

That was also probably the first time I realised that while I would be on stage, I would never be a Big M girl. It's not something that worries me now, but it's taken a lifetime to forgive myself for what I see as my perfectly capable, non–Big M girl body.

Thankfully, I've always been somewhat allergic to diets. By day two, the second day of the holidays and diet, I'd written absolutely nothing at all in my diary. It was over. My ability to stick to anything for too long fortunately meant I was back up at the local shops buying chips and gravy and ogling the poster on the deep-fryer of the gorgeous Chiko roll girl in her ripped shorts sitting astride a chopper motorcycle, provocatively holding a Chiko roll towards her mouth.

One of the wonderful things about my career is that I have been able to work through things that have shaped me later on down the track. Meeting Kenny was not the only person I loved as a kid who I was able to engage with in the documentary *Nice*. I also tracked down the original Chiko roll girl, Danielle Scandrett. I wanted to know what it was like being the object of everyone's desires while they waited for their deep-fried fish in batter and wondered exactly what was in the seafood extender.

Danielle the Chiko roll girl was exactly as you would imagine – clever and funny – and she looked back on that time in her life with the humour and pride that it deserved. It actually was a truly messed-up time where it was perfectly normal to use a scantily dressed woman to sell car tyres, a hot water system or shampoo.

How wonderful these days to see and hear women of all shapes, sizes, hair colour, skin colour, ethnicities and sexualities in our media, on our TVs and radios, on our movie screens and on our concert stages. We get to listen to what they say in podcasts and see them represent us in government. Little Myf would have been much the better if there had been more women upfront when she was growing up. But the magic of women like Dolly and Olivia still shines bright ... and, thanks to Olivia, I can still terrorise cats with my high notes and do a mean lap in the speed skating at the local rollerskating rink.

Little Red Corvette

(Prince Rogers Nelson)

6.

One day a prince will come

You know when you get those feelings? Not a sickly feeling in and around the stomach, but a little bit below that general area? I'm assuming you know what I'm talking about. We're all adults here. Yes ... *those* feelings. Those feelings that happened between tween and teen and made you feel as though you wanted to extend your hand (don't be filthy, I'm not going there) and touch the fingertips of the magical boy with the feathery mullet hairstyle, crop top and short shorts at the roller disco while Wham's 'Wake Me Up Before you Go-Go' blared out of the sound system. Those kind of sexy, romantic feelings. You remember them? You might still be having them. Lucky you.

I want you to cast your mind back, way back, to when those feelings started to rumble for the first time. Remember their warm, confusing tingle? And the sensation that you might just burst out of your own eyeballs if Bradley from the year above you at school offered you a chomp on his dim sim during recess. Not a euphemism!

When these feelings first came on for me, I didn't know what they were. But somehow, I knew they were something that should remain unspoken. Something I should keep to myself. They felt kinda wrong. Kinda naughty. Unknown yet incredibly enticing.

That was, until Prince came into my life.

Here was someone who embraced that yearning that I was beginning to feel around me; someone in the world of music, art and creativity, where I thought I wanted to be; but someone who was relatable too. He had the same raunchy, slightly curled shoulder-length hairstyle as my primary school teacher, Miss Chadwick, only he was wearing one single hoop earring instead of two like she did, gender boundaries be damned. How radical, I thought.

He teamed this with the lowest of cut v-neck t-shirts, showing a lot of chest and a hint of nipple, paired with the tightest of tight pants that were heaps tighter than the dark Fabergé stretch denim jeans my older brothers' friends wore when they went out every second Friday of the month to the blue light disco run by the local police. They'd come home sporting bruises on their necks and smelling of Alpine menthol cigarettes. And their jeans were tight.

Prince was singing something about wanting to be your lover. Love was a word that wasn't thrown around a lot in our house, we weren't that kind of family, so I was a bit confused. Love is what you wrote on Christmas cards or when you said goodbye, love is what you told someone you felt about them when you liked them, but what was this *lover* business? It was a term used to tease someone if they liked someone else at school. 'Ooooh, lovers,' we would say to those people, in jest. The word would usually elicit guffaws.

I wasn't alone in this somewhat fatal attraction. Prince's allure knew no bounds. Kit and I would obsess over every single new song he released. Here was a small man in extremely tight pants who looked straight down the barrel of the camera with a twinkle in his eye and would sing about seemingly adult, taboo things ... but it was more than that. He was an extraordinarily accomplished musician, with moves to die for, and who chose to be surrounded by kick-arse female musicians. Not too many acts made that kind of choice in the '80s. He also had a cheeky flicker behind the eyes that suggested that if you were different, you too could crack the code, to not give a fuck, to not care about being judged. When you're a kid, you just want to fit in, not stand out. Prince gave you permission to not fit in, to be different, and encouraged you to think that maybe not fitting in was kinda cooler. Here he was, giving us options when we hadn't known there were any.

Through Prince, I could smell freedom from what was increasingly feeling like the shackles of a small-town life. Prince offered me the option to want to be different. To forge my own path.

And he was certainly different from the blokes in my small town, who all had the same haircut and smoked the same cigarettes folded into their t-shirt sleeves and drank the same beers from a ring-pull can and drove the same Holden utes and listened to the same AC/DC songs (not that there's anything wrong with AC/DC, they were just popular with a certain type of male where I grew up). Prince was the stuff of a fantasy world, but it seemed accessible too.

The aforementioned blokes would also say Prince wouldn't last a day on the farm, but I knew he'd last a lifetime. In more ways than one.

To live in a small country town with only one main street down the guts of it, with not a lot of divergent paths to choose, meant having a glittery, glamorous man like Prince in my private life – who at the time was wearing his undies (in public, the shock!) matched with massively oversized shoulder-padded jackets and hairstyles with more product in them than a David Jones window display – was more than a bonus.

The song 'Little Red Corvette' sealed the deal for me. For the first time, he was singing about something little twelve-year-old me could relate to. (At this point, I hadn't quite worked out that it was about sex. I'm not sure what I thought it was about at first, it was just something different.)

Let's take the lyrics about driving to a place where horses run free.

At this time, like many twelve-year-old girls, I was mad for horses and had one of my own (thanks again, Uncle Neil). People kept telling me that my interest in horses would wane once I discovered boys, but that was yet to happen. You see, the thing is, Prince encouraged me to indulge in *both*.

And the man sang about jockeys!

I was small, Prince was small – I held dreams that I too could be a jockey, like Elizabeth Taylor in *National Velvet*. He understands me and my jockey dreams, I thought. If there's one thing about teen girls, it's that they want to be seen, and I felt *seen*.

When Prince sang about her having a pocket full of Trojans, some of them used, I was understandably confused but unperturbed. I hadn't quite come that far in my enlightenment and there was no such thing as Google to ask questions to, so I just assumed he was talking about something to feed the horse with.

As well as enabling my horse girl fantasies, Prince and his merry crew were a font of fashion inspo too. I copied the massive hairstyles of Wendy and Lisa from his band, using buckets of Taft hairspray that coated every surface of my bedroom, and possibly contributed to the hole in the ozone layer we were beginning to hear about. I wanted to be part of this magical musical world that offered not just sexiness, but extraordinary talent, pride, openness and inclusiveness. It was the absolute opposite of my country life, which I didn't even know I would eventually move away from. Prince, with his come hither looks, began to help prise the door open.

Eventually, I started to make the correlation between horses and hot things, Prince gave me the permission (my parents did not, soz, Mum and Dad) to go with these feelings and ask my first boyfriend to come and visit me at my house, on a Saturday night. This would require him to crawl silently, undetected by local dogs, through the vineyard near my house to meet me at the horse stables.

My excuse to my family about going to the horse stables at such a late hour was that I was going there to 'brush the horses'. Genius move from a clever teen right there. And to borrow from the immortal words of Prince, it was all right ... because it was a Saturday night. Permission had been granted.

It was inevitable then, that on that warm summer night, I would share an awkward pash with a boy with braces on his teeth and mud on his knees from crawling through the bushes, the still summer air heavy with the aroma of horse manure and the drone of mosquitoes. Now that's romance.

Three decades later, I heard Prince had died. I was saddened to hear of his untimely passing, an overdose of drugs that he'd struggled to wean off after hip surgeries. I had only recently attended his live performance where it was just him, a piano and a microphone. That concert was as extraordinary and as enlightening as you could imagine. Prince whizzing on to stage wearing children's sneakers with those light-up wheelie things on the bottom (I think he was like me and he bought his shoes from the kid's department because they fit better, and they're cheaper, of course). That night it was just him interpreting his own songs however he darn-well pleased. It was a masterclass from a musical genius.

His loss felt huge. I wasn't alone in feeling that. While I mourned his death like a friend, even though I knew really nothing of the real him, it was comforting to see his influence in everything still: in young artists influenced by his sound, in fashion, in the passion to create a world that is inclusive and beyond the norm. It's safe to say that, in death, Prince still lives. Which is really the way most of us want to go, right? Leaving a mark.

These days, relationships between fans and artists are often considered to be parasocial. That means that one person spends the time getting to know someone, while the other has no idea that's going on. With the access that social media has provided you could say that all fan–artist relationships now are parasocial. You can see inside artists' homes, what they're up to socially, watch them work and see what they're wearing at every event, where previously you'd know only what you'd read about them in magazines or the odd documentary on the TV. I didn't need to know anything about Prince's personal life to feel a connection, the music was enough.

When I hear Prince now it makes me happy. I remember little me, ready for the world to open, hungry for life and all its experiences. It reminds me to keep that belief in all possibilities, to maintain an excitement for the new, to be forever mischievous. Prince knew all this – he gave us this gift. And when I hear 'Little Red Corvette' I am immediately transported, overwhelmed by a heady mixture of lust and horse manure. It's an acquired taste.

One day, when the time is right, I promise to embrace a little bit more of Prince and have the guts to call someone my 'lover' without bursting into laughter.

Somewhere

(Leonard Bernstein and
Stephen Sondheim)

7.

Look to the edges

Around 1987, things in my life were really hotting up. Well, at least I thought so. I had my first job at the local Red Cliffs newsagent, selling newspapers, magazines, cigarettes and TattsLotto tickets. I'm pretty sure it wasn't legal for a fourteen-year-old to sell tickets to gamble, but as with advertising and punishing school children, the rules were a little looser then. I even sold a first division ticket to a local chap who was rumoured to have taken home over a million dollars. When he came back into the shop to buy more TattsLotto tickets with his winnings, he thanked me for being his good luck charm. I, of course, sensing an opportunity for profit, put out my hand with an added cheeky grin with the expectation of getting a tip for being such a charm. He shook his head, flatly refused, preferring to spend his winnings on not one but three Sportsgirl Barina hatchback cars, each with the signature Sportsgirl logo coloured stripe down the side of the car. Folk do things differently in Red Cliffs.

I loved working in a shop where I had magazines at my fingertips. An added bonus was that the mags that didn't sell on the shelf were removed, the covers cut off and sent back to the company for a refund. I got to take home the scraps (i.e. the rest of the mag), sans titles but otherwise intact. Every Saturday was like Christmas, as I'd take home a new *Dolly* or *Cosmo*, *Countdown* or *Smash Hits* magazine (sometimes all four!). TV had once been my lifeline to the outside world, now magazines also offered me the promise of a world filled with all the things I loved. Music, art, fashion, design. I was a young working woman with big dreams of having my hair permed and wearing a pastel business suit with shoulder pads *and* I was in magazine heaven. Life was good.

What I didn't enjoy about working at the newsagency was selling the porn mags. It was never comfortable for any of the parties involved. Not that I had any issues with the porn itself (who didn't look in amazement at a secret stash found in the shed at a friend's or uncle's house?), but the interaction between seller and purchaser was always awkward. Usually, the buyer was from another town. This was because the unspoken rule in those days was that if you were to buy porn, condoms, or anything of a sexual nature, you'd have to do so in a nearby town and not your own. Otherwise everyone would know what you were up to. So, when the strange men (in a small town you knew everyone) shuffled in, it was clear what they were shopping for. As I got older I made things even more awkward by not asking them if they'd like a paper bag with their copy of *Penthouse* and *Boobs Bonanza*. I'm a troublemaker at heart.

Working in the newsagent gave me a mainline to the high life. Or at least I thought it was the high life. I was working there with Lucinda, so we made our own fun. Being behind the counter meant we could get discounts on the snazzy pens in the special locked cabinet full of silver and gold Parker pens. This was particularly useful for boyfriends' birthdays, where I would go straight to the top shelf and get a discount on a writing tool that came in a snap-shut velour case. Très sophisticated. These days I can barely write with a pen, nor find one that works in that one drawer in the kitchen that houses all the detritus of life that you never use but think you might use one day. How times have changed.

At this point, I thought life in Red Cliffs on the weekend was pretty great. And it was. I wasn't dreaming too big just yet.

My Saturday mornings were spent working at the newsagent, then, in the afternoon, if it was summer,

I'd head off to the local tennis courts to participate in the weekend round robin competition. If it was winter, I'd play competition netball then go and watch the local team play footy on the adjacent oval. I didn't particularly excel at any sports (my mum, who I'll remind you was amazing at it and played hockey for Australia, said that I never had the fire in my eyes and, to be fair, she was absolutely right), but I enjoyed the team aspect of them all. In netball I played the position of wing attack. In netball speak this means I was not fast enough or didn't have enough flair to play the more glamorous centre, and I was forever resigned to calling out 'if you need' from the boundary of the two thirds of the court I was allowed in. Some say that you can tell the girl from her position on the netball court and I guess I was Wing Attack all the way. Running around making lots of noise and looking busy. Not super effective to the game, but happy to be involved for the good time. I knew in my heart, in a town and a family that was quite obsessed with sport, and of course, the arts too, that sport was not really my bag, I was more in the arts category. I was destined for other things. I hadn't quite worked out what they were yet, but my inadequacies on the court were outweighing my determination.

The job at the newsagent gave me sweet hard cash, the likes of which I'd never seen before. I now had money to buy something from the town's one fashion shop – the most gloriously '80s named Indimension, where I often ogled the acid wash jeans, the cable knit sweaters and Stuart Membery designer gear. It was on the main street, across the road from the newsagent, and I could now purchase the clothes that I loved rather than take them home 'on appro'. I'm not sure if 'on appro' is a term that's used anywhere else in the country, but we used to be able to take clothes home so Mum could give them the tick of approval (and pay later). I see now that this only happened because the woman who owned the shop knew everyone in town's mum, so she knew where you lived. I'll never forget the time Andre brought the most amazing skin-tight Fabergé cord jeans home on appro hoping Mum would say yes. They were so tight their cuffs flared out just a wee bit. We were in awe of those jeans. Mum, of course, said no, telling him the pants made him look like a pipe cleaner. Of course she was right.

There were other terms that seem to have been specific to my town because, to this day, when I use them I don't get the response I'm hoping for. The acronym JBF got thrown around among my friends a lot when describing bed hair, which we imagined might happen after someone had just had a fun time with someone else (which none of us knew *anything* about). As well, we called any type of white boot CFM boots, because we thought they were come hither boots of the worst kind. If anyone else can confirm or deny the existence of these acronyms outside of my town, it would be most appreciated.

With not much else to do in town, my weekends were full of sport and summer afternoons after school were spent at the local pool. I had dreams of becoming a competitive swimmer, only to have those dashed by the fact that, regardless of all the training I was doing, I was more of a reclining sea otter than a graceful swan. I settled on a different dream, that of an Olympic diver. Sadly, my backward somersault and forward half pike were not enough of a skill set to get me to the big pool, but it did give me a lot of time to ogle hot boy local swimmer as he trained for state team swim meets. While he trained, I lay on the blistering cement drying off my new racerback Speedos, eyeing him off, sucking provocatively on Big Boss lolly cigars and drinking from a can of Passiona. That's how it was done on the tellie, right?

Somehow, just somehow, hot state swimmer had started looking my way a few times (it must have been my fashionable mullet haircut that would dry out in such strange angles when left to its own devices), and when I offered him a taste from my packet of chicken Twisties, he said yes, and in no time we were doing partner bombs off the diving board and heading to the back of the pool grounds under the pine tree where the grass never grew.

My dream relationship came crashing down harder

than the tokens from a game of Connect Four. We're back at school. Hot country girl summer is very much over. Hot swimmer has turned colder than a Sunnyboy ice block and when I see him sharing his chicken Twisties with another girl, I'm devastated. Soon I found out that I'd been 'dropped', in the worst possible way. Via a note. Except that note didn't make its way to me directly – it made its way to me via the entire town. When you live in a country town of only a few thousand people, everyone knows what you're up to, and if someone writes a letter saying 'you're dropped' and then proceeds to actually drop it in the main street where someone finds it, it gets shared to supermarket cashiers, who pass it on to the manager, who shows it to your boss at the newsagency, who then passes it on to a teacher at your school to pass on to your mother, before she gives it to you. This was a humiliating public Facebook status update before such a thing existed. And the *humiliation* of a relationship status update from your mum is a teen's worst nightmare.

The fact that everyone in town knows your business isn't a bad thing when you need to be cared for by the community (it truly does take a village), but when you want a bit of teenage privacy to work out who you are and who you want to be, and to do some things that are downright naughty, the pull to seek adventure anywhere else is immense.

My weekend job made enough money for me to buy a ticket to my first-ever live music concert. I was beside myself. It was to take place on a footy oval, in the city that this time really was 'the big smoke' because it was the closest capital city – the booming city of Adelaide. My only experience of Adelaide before this was on family holidays. We'd sometimes stay at a place called Marineland Caravan Village in West Beach, which was directly under the flight path and next to a sewerage plant (so chic) and also not far from a mythical adventure park called Magic Mountain, which was a fake Uluru with waterslides coming out the sides (the disrespect of the '80s knows no bounds).

The gig was Australian singer Jimmy Barnes at Thebarton Oval. I was a mad Cold Chisel fan at this stage (it's a rural rite of passage to recite all the words to 'Flame Trees' at the end of a night out). 'Working Class Man' had been a phenomenal hit for the now solo Barnesy. The catch was, I had to hop on a bus from Mildura in the morning, travel for six hours to Adelaide, go to the gig, and then find my bus at the end of the show, at around midnight, to head home. It was almost a 24-hour round trip and I couldn't be more excited. I was getting out, sans parents, and seeing a proper live show with thousands of others, like I'd seen on the tellie. This was real adult stuff, and somehow I was allowed to do it.

Previously, very few live acts came to our neck of the woods, and if I had wanted to go, I hadn't been allowed to. Dipping back in to *The Judy Blume Diary* for a sec, there's an entire page dedicated to how much I hated my mum for not letting me go to the Irymple Leisure Centre to attend the blue light disco featuring two of the hottest Australian bands of the time, Wa Wa Nee and Geisha.

'I hate Mum, I hate Mum, I hate Mum, I hate Mum, I hate Mum,' I wrote as only a frustrated teen could.

It's not fair! She won't even let me go to the blue light. I hate her. She says I can go when I'm old enough, well when's bloody old enough? When I'm about 20 I will probably be able to go but I will be too old by then. It's a real big joke to you, Mum, isn't it? Well, I hate you very much.

Well, Mum and Dad, one day I'm going to do something that your [sic] not going to like, but do you think I care? No I don't. I will just tell you to go suck eggs you squares.

Oh, to be a parent of a teenager. Wouldn't wish it on my worst enemy.

But when the Barnesy gig came up and I asked if I could go, something had shifted in my folks and they deemed me old enough to finally get a taste of what I so deeply desired. So, with a few friends who'd also been given a leave pass, I got on that bus in my best outfit, which was a t-shirt from Sportsgirl that said 'Sportsgirl' on the front, and I was ready to take on the world.

And it was *amazing*! We shared Thebarton Oval with thousands of others, talked to strangers, warded off weirdos, took sips from a flagon of goon wine from someone nearby and, to be frank, saw absolutely nothing of the concert (given in those days the big screens weren't common and I'm five foot one, if I'm lucky). So while I loved every second, and thought I'd caught a glimpse or two of Barnesy and of guitarist Johnny Diesel's head, I saw very little of the actual performance. Strangely, it didn't dampen my enthusiasm for more. I bought a t-shirt as a souvenir and wore it to death with my button-up Levi 501 jeans and thought I was the coolest gal in town. I had been to a rock concert. The fire had been lit.

I wanted in on this music caper in some form or another. While I'd played piano most of my life, it was time to take things a little more seriously. This was a turning point.

The transformation from sport-loving, horse-riding country girl to serious music-loving young nerd was beginning. All it took was one teacher to get me over the line. Anne Dwyer is her name. She turned up at our high school from Melbourne, with a cool car and an expansive world view, and I couldn't get enough of what she was all about. She saw something in me at just the right moment, and she took it upon herself to guide me gently towards the things that could take me further, broaden my outlook and make me ask questions. She was also the first person to encourage me to play piano at a more academic level (even though I suspected I wasn't as naturally gifted as I thought), and she convinced me to study the theory of music too, which would inevitably help with my playing, as dull as it seemed at the time. She believed I could do it, which was something I didn't believe about myself. Everyone needs a teacher like Anne, and I feel very fortunate to have had her as an educator in my life. We still keep in contact today, and she and her partner, Don Collins, have continued to take on new challenges, always looking forward and learning. What a great role model for young me!

I decided to take music as a subject in year twelve (something no one at my high school had done before). There was a practical element (I was required to attend an exam at the end of the year in Melbourne – no pressure!) and a theoretical side. I never expected to enjoy this part so much – it was all about learning the theory behind Monteverdi's very first and early musical opera, *L'Orfeo*, through to Tchaikovsky's *Swan Lake* and Leonard Bernstein's *West Side Story*.

As an aside, I seemed to develop a rather unhealthy obsession with Leonard Bernstein around this time. The

more I learnt about him, the more enamoured I was
with his approach to music and life. He seemed to want
to share his passion for music, and his knowledge, to a
wider audience. His televised concerts were beamed out
to audiences worldwide, so everyone could join in and
enjoy. I loved this. His belief was that orchestral music
was for all, not just a select few. He also seemed utterly
besotted by what he was doing and keen to change the
world through supporting human rights, funding HIV/
AIDS research and advocating for nuclear disarmament
and world peace. His concert played on TV at the fall of
the Berlin Wall. *West Side Story* was particularly attractive
to teen me too – Bernstein took the format of musicals
(one I had struggled with a little up to this point), and
made music that, while incorporating more traditional
orchestral sounds, also delved into jazz and blues, which
made it far more relevant to a younger, more culturally
diverse audience, and me. *West Side Story* was a pretty hot
storyline – an updated (albeit '50s) *Romeo and Juliet* in
New York City. I gobbled it up. When Bernstein died
in his apartment in the New York Dakota building in
1990 (the same apartment building where John Lennon
was murdered ten years earlier) I held a little ceremony in
my bedroom, playing an illegally recorded tape I'd made
myself of *West Side Story* and other performances he'd
conducted, thinking deeply, as only a teenager can, about

his contribution to music. I think it's safe to say I was a bit of a weird kid, whose likes and taste were cherrypicked from whatever I could get my hands on at the time. If it had been today, I probably would have broadcast my ceremony and pain on a social media platform – thank goodness the internet didn't exist.

The song 'Somewhere (There's A Place For Us)' from *West Side Story* is eternally beautiful. A song of hope amid tragedy (when it's sung in the show Maria's brother has just died at the hands of her lover, Tony, and she weirdly forgives him). It's a duet that speaks of the two star-crossed lovers escaping to a place where they're far away from the trouble, where they're free to be themselves and in love. The words 'somehow', 'someday', 'somewhere' encapsulate the tragedy of impossible hope, and musically it taps into this knowing, borrowing a phrase from a slow movement of a Beethoven concerto and a longer phrase from the main theme of *Swan Lake*. It cleverly latches on to your heart and your head simultaneously in the most magnificent of ways.

As part of studying *West Side Story*, I headed over to Anne's house for a piano lesson and it was then that she decided I was ready for something new in my musical education. Anne played me a version of 'Somewhere' that would flip everything I knew about music. This version of the song sounded like it came from another planet. That planet was Tom Waits – the gravelly voiced American troubadour – who'd covered the song on his 1978 album *Blue Valentine.*

The song begins with sweeping orchestral strings, played for more of an emotional response than even Bernstein would think tasteful. Immediately I was hooked. And then there's that voice. What a voice. A low rumble that could have emanated from a drain on the side of the road. But it was beautiful. Utterly beautiful in its dissonance and opposition to the idea of what beauty was.

My skin tingled. My mind exploded. How did Waits change the meaning of the song from a tragic love ballad to a regretful lament, simply by interpreting it in his own unique way? How did he make this iconic song his own when it already had so much history? How did he make something so pure, so tragic, so perfect, even more interesting? Tom communicated musically that there is beauty in the margins, in the things that sound and look different, in the sounds off to the edges. This was a revelation. And it opened my mind to the knowledge that I should always look to the edges to find the gems others don't see. That song from Waits, given to me by my teacher, was a gift.

Wrote for Luck

(Paul Davis, Mark Day,
Paul Ryder, Shaun Ryder
and Gary Whelan)

8.

A whole lot confused

With Tom Waits now in my bag of musical goodies, I was ready for the next step – university. I auditioned for a place in Melbourne University's Music Education course and miraculously got in. The year was 1991. I packed my favourite outfit, a pair of khaki dress shorts (to the knee, of course) with a tan belt to complete the dull look and sensible slip-on shoes. I was dressing in that very '90s normcore way that I thought made me look rather classy, like a sophisticated Country Road lady but, in reality, had me looking like I was about thirty years older than I was. My advice now is to enjoy your teenage years, kids, don't try and dress like your mum, it's your time to shine!

At the ripe old age of seventeen, going on eighteen, I was all set to move to Melbourne. The goal was to move in with Andre and Kit into a share house in the suburb of Parkville, near the uni, and to become the pianist I'd always dreamt of being. Or a music teacher. Either or; I wasn't fussed. Things didn't work out quite as I'd imagined though. I was in Melbourne and I was about to have my world blown open. And, in hindsight, it was for the best.

I hadn't anticipated the level of skill and talent I would be studying beside in the music course. Quite a few of the students had only got a place after spending two years studying a jazz improvisation course at a specialised music TAFE, which was used as a way to gain entry if you didn't get through the first audition like I did. My repertoire of a little bit of Mozart here, a little bit of Bach there, wasn't quite up to scratch. I suspect I may have been accepted into this highly competitive course on a 'country quota' because they had to have a certain percentage of country kids to make up the numbers. I can't confirm this, but so many of the other students had done part or all of that course, and there I was with just a few tunes under my belt and a whole load of optimism.

On the first day, as I sat with the other thirty students who would be in my year, I could see that my name had been written down on the class list not as Myfanwy but as Myfanny. When this was read out in front of the class, everyone laughed and from that moment my nickname was My Fanny, which, if you're American is fine, it just means 'my arse', but in Australia it's referring to the vulva and that, my friends, is never not funny, except to the person it involves, which was me. I have a particular friend who took this naming one step further after this unfortunate episode, calling me at every opportunity the delightfully hilarious My Fanny Wart Hurts. Read it slowly, you'll wanna scratch yourself afterwards. Also, LOL. Unless your name is Myfanwy Warhurst.

Not surprisingly, I found the first year of university quite difficult. When you add learning to live out of home and cook and clean for myself, it was a lot to cope with. Our whole house was pretty ordinary at the maintenance part of life. At least every few weeks someone refused to wash the dishes that had piled up and we ended up taking them outside and hosing them down to get the mould off. We were gross university students living the dream. I'd mastered how to make bolognaise sauce with a recipe from Mum, and that was all I needed.

I was also getting used to socialising at pubs with a fake ID provided by my brother's friend. It was a learner licence permit. They used to be simply a piece of paper with no photo, making them excellent to use when you were under-age. The kids have got it so much tougher these days, what with everything online and documented, and they've all got phones so parents can keep tabs on them. It's harder to do anything naughty. That's why they're so well behaved in comparison to our generation. Some of my friends' kids behave even better than their parents do now.

Another thing I found increasingly difficult about the course was the amount of practice I had to do on the piano just to keep up with the rest of the class. I'd had my upright piano from home delivered to the terrace house we were living in, and it sat smack-bang in the hallway just near the front door. It was too big and too heavy to go anywhere else. It meant I couldn't shut the door on a practice room and focus. That was my excuse, anyway.

I also realised pretty quickly I wasn't up to scratch technically. I could sightread music, but not at the pace that other class members seemed to do without faltering. Coming from a small high school where I was up near the top of the class (not hard when there were only twenty-five students in my whole year) having to accept that this new me was a bit of a struggler didn't sit well.

What I was good at, however, was socialising. I loved meeting new people and felt like there were a few people in my course I'd like to get to know better. So I thought it was up to me to encourage some further bonding, if you like. Most of the students I was studying with lived in Melbourne and still lived at home with their folks (except for the mature-age students, who looked upon us young ruffians with the disdain we deserved). Having my own house was considered quite a novelty. So it was decided, or at least, I decided, I'd have a party. What could go wrong?

Around that time, I'd also discovered Melbourne public radio station Triple R and the national youth station Triple J, so my musical world was quickly expanding. I had a boom box with requisite CD player in the lounge room and, in those days, if you had a party, you didn't have a DJ or a Spotify playlist, you just played what you had. I already had a well-worn copy of Neneh Cherry's *Raw Like Sushi* record (I was obsessed with her, and took great pride in reciting the rap from the iconic 'Buffalo Stance', I'm ashamed to say because frankly I must have looked like a complete dick!). I wanted to desperately show how hip and cool I was becoming with my new CDs and knew that my new edgy records would get the dancefloor pumping. Maybe not in the same way as Black Box's 'Ride on Time' or Technotronic's 'Pump Up the Jam' always do; I mean, who doesn't put down their bottle of Sub Zero and fight their way through the crowd to hit the floor when the opening refrains of these songs start? But there was something a little edgy about the direction in which I was going. The beats were different, the sounds were less dance around your handbag and more angular and, dare I say, euphoric.

The first of them was the Happy Mondays' *Pills 'n' Thrills and Bellyaches*, with hits like 'Kinky Afro', 'Step

On' and 'Loose Fit'. I'd heard about this group from Manchester in the UK on a regular Saturday night at home watching the SBS world movie channel (guaranteed nudity, guaranteed adult themes equals excellent viewing for a teenager trapped at home, but more on that later) and flicked over for the start of the ABC's *Rage* which, I think we can safely say, was the original music video show at a time when there was no YouTube. *Rage* was the only way you could see new and old music videos. It was pot luck what sort of videos you'd get, but invariably you'd stay awake, waiting for the next one, and the next, to see if something took your fancy, and you'd be tired but stuck in the beanbag craving just one more good song before bed.

I saw the Happy Mondays clip back home in Red Cliffs, in the same lounge room where I would copy the moves on a Jane Fonda workout video on a daily basis, in the faint hope that I still had a chance of growing a set of pins like Barbarella herself. Note to self: legs don't lengthen after a certain age. My interests changed instantly from fitness and leotards to craving a rather more hedonistic lifestyle. The song was 'Wrote For Luck' and the clip featured a young man, in a club, surrounded by people, dancing with what looked like abandon, all completely blissed out. What I was watching was a rave. Something I'd read about in magazines but never witnessed in person. The repetitive, mesmerising dance beat of acid house dragged me in, and

I stayed for the absolute freedom that this scene promised me. Now I know that the men I saw – singer Shaun Ryder and the group's vibe man, Bez – were completely off their chops on ecstasy, yet they were clearly living their best lives. It looked like a life I wanted in on.

As soon as I could – which was when I got to Melbourne, because none of this stuff was available in Mildura – I bought the group's latest CD. And, oh man, now that was an education. This in turn led me to New Order, which led me to Joy Division, and the Manchester music scene based around Tony Wilson's Factory Records and the near mythical Hacienda nightclub and acid house.

The normcore dressing would have to go, I thought, to evolve into something more edgy, which really just turned into me being slightly confused in my Doc Marten eight-ups (that's all about the holes for laces, and eight-ups were *kewel*) matched with a black cheesecloth top, beads and stripey leggings. Clearly, I was mixing my styles – a little bit rave, a little bit punk, a little bit goth and a whole lot confused.

I knew absolutely nothing about the drugs, like ecstasy, that fuelled this burgeoning scene at this stage. Weird, given where I'd grown up, which was commonly known at the time as the Grass Capital of Victoria. Mildura in the '80s was a notorious Calabrian mafia stronghold, with a series of mafia murders in the area, one shooting even taking place on a property that looked onto the back of our high school. I distinctly recall one particular night where a police helicopter flew above our property, and surrounding ones, searchlight on high beam, looking for drugs growing between the vines. I also remember when one of our regular big gamblers on TattsLotto at the newsagency came in to put on his bet and struggled to do so with a hand that was freshly missing a finger. And when my brother's friend's dad mysteriously disappeared to Italy, never to be seen again, we all knew why. A lot of bad stuff happened in our town, and yet no one ever really spoke about it.

But the Happy Mondays weren't Calabrian mafia. They clearly took drugs with abandon and were sparkling with pure joy and pleasure (although meeting them years later, I witnessed the toll the drugs had taken on them, even though they'd cleaned up their act decades earlier).

So with my Happy Mondays CD and Primal Scream's *Screamadelica* – another UK acid house beat, rock and roll, and soul melange that sounded unlike anything else in the world to me, it might as well have come from outer space – I was ready to party.

I'd never hosted a party of my own like this before so I was a little worried about how my two groups of friends would get along. First, I had my friends I'd made through my brother, Kit, and some friends from my home town who also lived in Melbourne, and second, my new, rather more buttoned-up uni music friends who were mostly pretty nerdy and probably wouldn't understand the debauchery that the others were capable of. It was a suck-it-and-see problem.

There's nothing that can quite prepare you for the chaos of young people at a party where all bets are off, there are no parents, and more than half don't know how to handle their alcohol. My main memory of that night was that the guy I was thinking I might be keen on drank so much he left me mid-conversation to bolt up the stairs towards the toilet. He then proceeded to open the door of the toilet (there was no lock) without considering that there might be someone sitting on the toilet at that exact moment. He then vomited between the legs of a classmate as they sat on the loo doing their own business. Can you imagine how horrific that would be? Did this scare me off said fella? Not at all. I've always tried to see the good in people.

Other memorable moments included realising that the clothes dryer had been used by someone to store booze because they didn't feel they could protect their drinks stashed in the bath from tightarse uni students (fair call) and the awfulness of having to explain that to the non-family housemate whose dryer was now full of melted ice. Another was my brother's friend, Cahal, who made the most of his extra year of drinking experience trying to teach me how to make myself vomit to feel better because

I wasn't feeling too great. Sadly, I failed at most of this task but I was glad to have learnt this skill.

My disparate worlds collided successfully that night and even the guy who vomited on someone else (and I won't name him, because he's a respectable gent these days) is still part of our friendship group. We danced the night away to my three CDs and friendships were forged that night that have also lasted until this day. I was pleased because I'd shored up my position as the uni course's Julie (the cruise director from *The Love Boat* whose job was to organise the social functions and all the fun). This sat extremely well with me at the time. I liked the feeling of belonging in a world that felt so sparkly and new.

There was one problem though. I was drowning at uni. I couldn't keep up. The hours of practice I needed to do per day just to get to the bare minimum level was killing me. I loved being at uni, but I was flailing, and possibly failing. I was a terrible accompanist on the piano – this is something a piano player must be good at. My sightreading wasn't quick enough and, looking back now, I didn't understand enough about how music worked. I wasn't going to be able to do more than just scrape through my first year. I was winning socially but floundering academically.

As I neared the end of the year, with the knowledge that some pretty ordinary marks were coming my way,

I knew it was time to make a tough decision. I finished the year (I passed, but barely) and decided to ditch the music course and cross over to complete a Bachelor of Arts. My dad, who is one of the most creative people I know yet hilariously still questions the value of the arts, was known to jokingly call a BA a degree in Bugger All. And yes, a BA is a course for those who don't know what they want to do, but for me, at that particular time, it was a godsend. All I wanted to do was learn about the world, about art, architecture, film, history, politics, critical theory and the buzzword at the time: postmodernism. I was salivating over this stuff. The music course had a framework of reference that was too narrow for my eager mind, and I wasn't great at playing. So getting myself a degree in Bugger All was the best thing for me.

I eventually narrowed my field a little more and majored in fine art theory, leading to post-grad research in art curatorial studies. At the end of it all I genuinely thought I would be a curator, swanning around an art gallery somewhere (which had a lot to do with another of my great loves – architecture – as big galleries are usually housed in fabulous buildings).

While I was studying arts, my heart was pulling me back to music, albeit in a different way. I was going to gigs night after night in Melbourne, venues like the Punters Club and The Evelyn. I started writing about these gigs for a local street press magazine called *Inpress*, a publication that came out every Wednesday morning, highlighting all the gigs you could see that week. Again, pre-internet, the role of these publications can't be underestimated. Getting a by-line in there, well, that was just crazy talk. But somehow I did it! I started writing gig reviews. The payoff was that I'd get free entry to any gigs. Living on no money, this was a huge deal. And I could take a friend. If it all happened on dollar-pot night (that's a dollar for a glass of beer) it was the greatest and cheapest night ever.

I would eventually work as the music editor for *Inpress*, where I was in charge of all the music editorial content that went into the mag, and the writers who contributed, so it was truly a formative period in my evolution. At the time though, I just enjoyed having my name on the door at cool venues, and feeling like I was starting to really get to know this town that initially had seemed so insurmountable.

Eventually I moved out of the share house with my brothers, choosing instead to forge a path of my own with my new friends. Andre and Kit remained in our close group of friends. To this day, our friendship groups are intertwined. I feel very lucky to have spent these formative years sorting out who I was while in my brothers' company. They were never judgemental or critical of the choices I made, but they were always there if I needed them.

And we still saw loads of each other. We would all gather on a regular basis to watch Kit and Andre (who by then were legitimate musicians in Melbourne) playing in their band Manic Suede at a venue in Collingwood called The Club. This venue was dangerous because it was open all hours and took all comers. The band started at 2 am. These days I couldn't even muster up a 10 pm start time, such is my age, but 2 am seemed perfectly normal back then. As did the million mixed drinks I'd consume. I would have finished my shift at the pub, where I also worked pulling beers, and was ready to party. And party we did. Every single Friday night!

It was around this time that I established friendships with so many of my dearest friends. Here I met Katrina, who'd grown up in the suburb of Brunswick, who was now living upstairs above one of the bars in Fitzroy (this location was essentially like striking gold in those days). She loved her rock and roll and metal and had funny tales of being a metal chick in Brunswick in the '80s. We immediately bonded. Kit and his best friend, Tim Ross (who he'd met by chance on an open day for his uni course after fainting and Tim coming to his aid), had a couple of share houses that were the sites of some of the most disgraceful behaviour a twenty-something can muster. Their first place was an old office building that had been adapted into a residence but clearly not quite to code, because it came complete with a tiny windowless office kitchen that was forever covered with dirty dishes, and a mouldy basement permanently filled with water. They dubbed the place Club 612, due to its address on Queensberry Street, North Melbourne.

The parties at 612 were legendary, and I spent many an early morning sleeping off a big night on their lounge-room couch, which was really a stolen high jump mat. That was probably the most useful piece (and most appropriate) of their furniture because it was comfortable and easy to hose down. Tim was honing his comedy skills during this time, while Kit was working on his music, but their shenanigans were all driven by fun rather than potential careers, which in hindsight made for moments of pure joy. It was in this house that they formed the band Black Rose, a fictional Oz rock tribute band that was referencing the bloated rock of the '80s way before the '80s had become fashionable again. The premise was that they would all play instruments that they couldn't play, and Tim would sing their imagined classic hits like 'I Drive a Holden, My One's a Brown One' (a tribute to the great Australian car and bogan Oz rock) and 'Fast Times at Black Rose High'. Kit had never played the drums before this, and this joke led to him becoming a fantastic drummer who would become a member of garage rock band Rocket Science years later. Kit is now known as much for his incredible drumming as he was for his guitar playing and TV music making.

At this time I lived in various share houses, too many to mention. One in particular felt like a mansion because I lived in what I glamorously called a self-contained extension (it weirdly had a kitchen sink and a shower, and nothing else but a few oddly joined tiny rooms) of an old terrace house in West Melbourne. My friend Georgie lived out the back in what we called the shed, because that's literally what it was, a shed. Freezing and falling apart, it backed on to a lane where people would regularly have sex after exiting from the pub on the corner. It was rough, but we didn't care a jot! My dear friend Beth, also originally from Mildura, lived upstairs in the best room, with a balcony that fronted the street, as all those beautiful old terrace houses do, and our friends Chico and Nat had the bedrooms downstairs. It was a happy household that functioned as well as a house full of people with no money and lots of spare time could.

Georgie worked part time up the road at a shop called Not Quite Right, which did what it says on the packet; it sold everything that had just gone out of date or had come from a damaged shipping crate from a country you'd never heard of. We loved that she worked there because, being poor students, how else were we going to afford a nice cheese or an exotic chocolate bar? Georgie's arrival home after work with a bag of goodies was always met with great excitement. Cheeses that were illegally out of date were ours to indulge in (if you're getting the stuff that needs to be thrown out from a shop that sells out-of-date stuff already, meant it must have been pretty bad, but cheese is already mouldy, right?). And the weird exotic biscuits from Russia or Azerbaijan were always a household favourite.

We spent our nights partying in our lounge room located upstairs, appropriately adorned with a *Reservoir Dogs* poster and The Cure's poster for their record, *The Head On the Door*. I think it's safe to say that every student house had a *Reservoir Dogs* poster on their wall in the '90s, and a copy of the soundtrack, which set the tone for a decade of amazing film soundtracks.

I had my twenty-first birthday party in that house, the upstairs lounge filled with so many people the old wooden floor was bouncing when my parents came to wish me well. Fortunately, that meant that Mum and Dad didn't want to venture any further (probs mostly for safety reasons and because they couldn't see through the smoke). Funnily enough, I was never really a fan of marijuana, I do love the medicinal properties of it but, personally, it made me anxious. However, a friend decided that they would give me a lovely twenty-first birthday present, which was a batch of cookies. Now these weren't cookies of the Anzac variety, these were special cookies, ones that would make you cooked. So, I decided I would set them aside, on my bedside table, to give to whomever wanted them the next day. My beautiful dog, Elly, who I will mention at this point lived to a ripe and healthy age of seventeen, decided that she was a dog and she should do her dog business and eat something she shouldn't. They were just sitting there for the taking. The next morning, hungover and seedy, the members of our household stepped carefully around the empty cans that were strewn all over the joint, to converge in the lounge room and dissect the night before. Something was amiss. Our favourite house member (when is a dog not the best house member of any house? I defy you to suggest otherwise) hadn't joined us. Usually Elly was wherever I was; she and I were joined at the hip. We looked down the stairs to see little Elly, a courageous Kelpie Heeler cross who'd lived her best life thus far after being adopted from the Lort Smith Animal Hospital, looking up at us, glazed expression, unable to take any steps up the steep stairs. Oh darl, I thought, we've all been there. Fortunately, after a hasty call to the vet, who suggested that we keep an eye on her and make sure she didn't pass out, we were told that she would be perfectly fine by the next day. The vet then said, don't worry, this happens all the time. Like I said, Elly survived. Thankfully. And she especially enjoyed the whole pizza that she stole later that night from our home delivery.

Living in West Melbourne was my gig monster training ground. Our household would all go out to gigs, and whenever Black Rose performed we would dress up as their groupies, naming ourselves The Rosettes. We enjoyed dressing up in our '80s gear as well, ironically of course. I was by now working at the local pub up the road in North Melbourne and nights would be spent there, then after I clocked off I'd go to see a band or two at indie dance night Clockwork Orange, where people would dance like Morrissey to Smiths songs. Every night was a different adventure, a wonderful time of learning who we were and how to express ourselves in the adult world. Inevitably, we would head home, often ending up at the 24-hour Embassy Taxi Cafe, conveniently located across the road on our street in West Melbourne. We would be served by the same woman night after night, her comfortingly creased face etched by years of nightshift and dealing with drunks all the while smoking endless cigarettes behind the counter. That taxi cafe still stands today, its interior updated in the 2000s I suspect, although some of the menu items, like ham steak and pineapple, remain, a nod to a different and much simpler era of convenience food. I still dream about the bog standard, old-school, no-frills burger with the lot from this joint that touches the memory buds as much as it does the tastebuds. They really don't make burgers like they used to, except here.

Sadly, the familiar, comforting face of the smoking lady behind the counter is no longer there.

Life in West Melbourne was so fun, for the next few years I stayed in the area, living in various old terrace houses with friends, working at local restaurants and bars like The Public Bar in North Melbourne, while studying and writing those gig and arts reviews for the local street press before getting my job there as the music editor. My tastes were expanding too. I was getting into electronic music, obsessing over records by Massive Attack and later, DJ Shadow's ground-breaking album of instrumental hip hop and samples and, at the same time, relishing in much heavier sounding stuff. I could be seen regularly front row at a Kim Salmon and the Surrealists residency at The Tote or watching his other dirty rock and roll group Beasts of Bourbon, or bowing at the majesty of filthy rockers the Powder Monkeys. I could also be found at a random rave in a warehouse in Collingwood or the Docklands. I was so lucky to have such extensive and great music at my fingertips at a time when the Australian music scene was expanding and experimenting.

I hadn't really made many friends in the arts courses I was doing. The enrolment levels of such a broad degree made it difficult to see or meet with anyone on a regular basis. I was starting to think I was a bit of a loser in the academic realm, until I recognised a familiar face one day in one of my film studies tutorials.

I'd seen Steph before at a rock and roll music night at a notorious nightclub, Hard 'N' Fast at Chasers. I knew that she was in a local indie band, Sandpit, that I liked. We bonded over a love of schlocky films, music, popular culture and visual arts. While everyone else in film class was keen to dissect Fellini's critically lauded black-and-white arthouse masterpiece based on his childhood experiences, *Otto e Mezzo*, Steph and I chose to write a tute paper on the role of the 'final girl' in horror movies like *The Texas Chainsaw Massacre* (hint, she was the one who never had sex – moralistic much?). We got through the course at the same pace (she, too, followed the curatorial studies path but also found herself a life in music) and around 1996, after we'd both completed our Honours in Fine Art Degree and were about to embark on our postgrad studies, we moved into a house together in the suburb of Collingwood. Steph was a musician and worked part time at the terminally cool but sadly now defunct Polyester Records in Melbourne while I was working at *Inpress*. We thought we were so grown up and posh in our two-bedroom terrace located right next to the meeting of one of the busiest roads in Melbourne (Punt) and the Eastern freeway, mostly because it had fresh carpet, proper curtains and, the piece de resistance, a dishwasher; a first for both of us.

During this time, Steph met her now partner, Paul Dempsey, who was fronting his group Something for Kate, a group who seemed to be destined for great things, according to the press at the time. And for good reason. Paul is to me, an extraordinary talent with a voice that somehow has a direct line to the listener's emotions. Steph joined Something for Kate too. Eventually, Paul moved into our house. Many a late night was spent sitting around on the carpet (we hadn't graduated yet to purchasing couches, and the ones we eventually did get were a brown velour duo from the Salvos), drinking red wine and discussing the state of the world, as all good twenty-somethings are wont to do.

We solved very few problems, but we did dissect Radiohead's *OK Computer* album to within an inch of its life, spilled glass upon glass of cheap red cask wine on the once fresh carpet, then poured a lot of salt on top to soak it up. This handy tip was gleaned from a Country Women's Association book of tips on how to deal with all sorts of stains. Sadly, we didn't have a vacuum cleaner to vacuum up these hefty piles of salt that slowly turned pink, so our lounge room was starting to look more like an ant farm than a liveable abode.

I didn't care, I was living the bigger life I had wanted when I was growing up in Red Cliffs. They weren't just happy Mondays in that house ... almost all the days were happy.

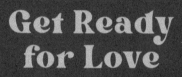

Get Ready for Love

(James A Sclavunos, Martyn Paul Casey,
Nicholas Edward Cave and
Warren Lee Ellis)

9.

Radio days

As we came to the end of the year 1999, the very year Prince had sung about, I had survived the '90s and was happily partying like it truly was the end of the world. There was every chance it might be. This fictional moment in song was writ large in front of us all, and all we could talk about was the damage that might ensue should our clocks and computers go bonkers at the strike of midnight because a rumoured Millennium Bug was set to wreak havoc. With all the class I could muster, I did my bit and brought in the new millennium at a massive rave called Welcome 2000 at the barren Docklands in Melbourne (before they were developed into a now still-windswept area full of apartments). If you believe in the old adage, 'Start the new year as you want to proceed', then mine didn't start particularly well at all as most of it was spent with my head in a wheelie bin, after overindulging in all the fun the night had promised.

My life had taken a rather interesting turn in the years prior to this celebration. I'd gone from thinking I would become an art curator of sorts, doing a bit of writing on the side, to flipping the tables completely and choosing my new love, radio. It was a topsy-turvy but extremely fun few years, and my flip was leading me towards a career that was less defined, but far more suited to me. At first it felt slightly directionless, full of possibility yet narrow in potential. I was living through a whole world of 'what ifs?', with no real answers in sight. But I went in this new direction with enthusiasm and, though I didn't know it at the time, it was exactly the right path for me.

Your twenties are a wildly confusing time. It's a period when you're fending completely for yourself, as you should – you're an adult and the responsibility for your life rests solely on your shoulders. And yet, you're still working out who you are, who your friends are, what you want from life, and, of course, wanting to do all the partying that you can. I did all of these things. Times ten. Hence the head in a wheelie bin. Thank goodness we didn't have cameras on our phones back then because this would have been a fun pic that could be used to blackmail me with later.

By around 1998 I was heavily ensconced in the Melbourne music and arts scene. I had moved up and

ABOVE: My dad as a bub with his mum, Ruby, and his dad, Abel. Ruby's mum was Maud, the subject of my episode of *Who Do You Think You Are?*

RIGHT: Mum and me.

Dad, Kit, Mum and me, photographed by the *Donald Times* upon our arrival in Donald, for an article alerting everyone that there was a new school principal in town.

A Warhurst family portrait. Just look at the boys' matching Miller shirts. How cool.

ABOVE: Me, Kit, Andre and Shaun up at the block in the tin shed that housed us . . . and the snake. Darling View, New South Wales.

LEFT: 'Go to your room and draw a horse.' Note my Miss Piggy 'Pig Power' poster in the background. An early inspiration.

Me, displaying my early modelling career poses in front of the family tram.
Not sure what the dog is doing.

Me and two of our family pets in front of our mud-brick house, built by us in Red Cliffs.

TOP: What a difference a few years make: from a teen debutante in pearls to a midriff-baring, music-obsessed twenty-year-old.

MIDDLE LEFT: My first party in my first share house with my brother Kit and Tim Ross, 1991.

ABOVE: With my school friend Lucinda at our school social, channelling a Madonna *La Isla Bonita* fashion moment in my matador-style dress.

LEFT: *Inpress* days with the then editor, Darren Fishman, at the Big Day Out, maybe 1995.

TOP: Saturday nights are all right.
Presenting the Net 50 chart show on Triple J.
Note the reel-to-reel player behind me!

MIDDLE: When Prime Minister Julia Gillard came
along to our Spicks and Speck-tacular show –
with my two favourites, Adam Hills and Alan Brough.

LEFT: *Spicks and Specks* dress-ups were always a hoot.
Alan and I both imitating Amy Winehouse, obviously
before she passed away.

With my Spicks and Speck-tacular touring family, Kit, Liv Boyle, Gus Agars, Georgia Chadwick, Alan Brough, Adam Hills and Stevie Hesketh.

LEFT: Double J afforded me the chance to meet many of my heroes. Neneh Cherry was a big one of mine.

ABOVE: That face when you meet your hero, Kenny Rogers.

TOP: With my beautiful Bang Fam, James Findlay, Zan Rowe and Meagan Loader.

MIDDLE: With my darling co-host, Joel Creasey, on our first stint as Eurovision commentators in Ukraine, 2017.

LEFT: When in Russia on assignment in the snow, always accessorise with local hairy men.

Who doesn't love a green-and-gold sequinned tracksuit?
Eurovison is the gift that keeps on giving, as far as I am concerned.

Me, just before I went into camp to
participate in *I'm A Celebrity . . . Get Me
Out Of Here!*, and already terrified as I'm
standing next to a sleeping cheetah in the
wild. Little did I know that things would
only get more terrifying.

In Paris in 2022 . . . I have more to
do and definitely more songs to hear,
but I can honestly say, up to this point,
I have had the time of my life!

was now the managing editor at *Inpress*. I had a team of wonderful staff working with me (most of whom I am still friends with today). You never forget the camaraderie of your first work friends, and we were a formidable group. I think it's safe to say we loved the adrenaline of putting the mag out each week, drunk on the power of deciding which pics were included in the club photos section and making up the weekly horoscope. I was working as hard as I was socialising, as my role meant showing up to gigs, shows, theatre, and being seen to be a part of the scene. Which I didn't mind at all. I was also responsible for putting together a fresh magazine every Monday so it was on the street first thing Wednesday morning. That part was particularly hard, especially after a full weekend. But I loved it all.

Deadline days are always high pressure, that doesn't change no matter what your job, but they were even harder back in the '90s when the paper had to be printed out on photographic paper and cut and pasted on a page before it could be sent off to the printers. The margin for error was huge. An article could literally fall off, unnoticed, on the way to the printers, and you'd have a blank page; or the wrong thing could be pasted in a space and be missed by exhausted eyes. As computers improved, and the printing process developed, deadlines became less fraught.

In the very early days of my time at the magazine, the pressure to meet deadline was often made worse by a member of the team who would throw a tantrum in the office, again usually after a big weekend, where furniture would sometimes be thrown and much yelling would ensue. It happened on a weekly basis and we were terrified. This type of behaviour would not be tolerated today but, back then, it was perfectly normal. I'm glad times have changed.

Another normal thing back then was having meetings at our desks where people were encouraged to smoke while talking with you. A full ashtray meant there had been a full day of meetings. If you thought *Mad Men* was a long-gone '60s fantasy, I can tell you that aspects of that lifestyle were still to be found in '90s Melbourne office life.

Gigs were always full of smoke. It was only when smoking was banned at venues that we all realised how truly disgusting we were. Suddenly, the unwashed hair, the bad breath, farts and burps of every person could be distinguished, where previously they were hidden behind a cloud of toxic puff. It was almost as bad as the time I went to a gig during what was known as the Melbourne gas crisis, where the city's gas supplies were cut off for two weeks in 1998 after an accident at the Longford Gas Plant. I don't remember who was playing, but I do remember the stench. Legendary venue the Corner Hotel was packed with a thousand unwashed Melburnians (most young folk and students' houses were on gas because it's cheaper), so the pong of everyone's dank greasy hair, and poorly washed bodies overpowered the smell of patchouli or nag champa incense they'd burnt to cover it. It was like in the Middle Ages, where everyone probably should have been holding some sort of potpourri container near their nether regions. We were rank. The entire city was rank. Ah, the '90s.

During my time at *Inpress* I enjoyed some great perks. I had the magnificent opportunity to see all the touring acts and local acts I could, and I lapped it all up. To me, this was my second university degree. I was out at least five nights a week. It was also a time when record companies had money to spend and most of us were naive about the nature of the industry (which has faced a serious and extremely timely reckoning over the last few years, particularly in the light of #metoo allegations, of which there are too many to mention). Back then, those things were still just whispered rumours, and the egos grew and the money flowed. There were free tickets, free dinners and fun promo opportunities galore.

It was also a time when everything felt like it was happening for the first time – hip hop was beginning to explode on a global scale, dance/electronic music had become a serious force in a commercial sense, indie rock was having a revival and Australian music was enjoying huge success locally and overseas. It was such an exciting time to be a part of the Australian music industry and I loved it. I remember in the very early 2000s being invited to a cheeky burger dinner at the Espy followed by tenpin bowling with a yet to be globally massive New York indie band called The Strokes; watching the 'are they or aren't they brother and sister?' group (we still didn't know at this stage) The White Stripes play to a hundred people at my friend Elise's basement bar The 9th Ward in the city; and the night the big label bosses who'd flown in from all over the world turned up at the gig of a little-known rock band called Jet, at the Prince Patrick Hotel, in an effort to sign the hottest band in the world at the time. It was a feeding frenzy. They were offered a deal that night and the rest, as they say, is history.

Living in the inner city, I spent most nights at a bunch of pubs in a small radius in the north of Melbourne to see music – the Punters Club (once legendary for cultivating Melbourne's burgeoning music scene), The Tote (still going, still legendary), The Evelyn and The Rochester.

The Melbourne Comedy Festival, as it was called then, was also establishing itself as a world-class festival, and some of my friends were involved in Melbourne's blossoming comedy scene. I whiled away many an eve laughing at the Prince Pat in Collingwood or on Sundays at the Espy in St Kilda. I was a veritable human gig guide when it came to knowing what was on, where, and who the up-and-comers were. I prided myself on this at the time.

It was through these comedy connections that I got my first big radio break.

Kit's friend Tim, had started doing stand-up with a mate of his, Merrick Watts, and together they later became the duo Merrick and Rosso. All of our friendship group spent a wild few years in the '90s trying to scrape through uni, living in terrible share houses in North and West Melbourne, making short films, putting on comedy shows and performances – and it was a brilliant training ground for what was to come.

At one point, with my housemate Georgi Herrick and Tim's then girlfriend Loren, we even self-produced a theatre show for the Melbourne Fringe Festival. The show was called *Makeup*, and it was all about subverting society's expectations of women, in our very '90s, grunge queen way. Part of the show involved Georgi reading from a novel she'd written when she was a child about INXS's Michael Hutchence falling in love with her while spending a summer at her parents' holiday house in Lorne, Victoria (it's hilarious, in fact, maybe the publishers should have given eleven-year-old Georgi a book deal, not me!). At one point in the show I did a reverse striptease to a Tom Waits song to show the world that I was more than just the girl who sold your beers (I still worked in a bar at that time). Very deep. Performance art, we deemed it, and performance art it was. In hindsight, it was probably amateurish at best, but we were loving ourselves sick. We even managed to get an article in *The Age* newspaper, which was huge for us at the time, the journo probably as baffled as we were about the messages we were trying to convey.

I watched Merrick and Rosso's rise in popularity with pride. Our friendship group had watched them perform hundreds of times and loved seeing the rest of the country start to latch on to their very special, and hilarious, comedic friendship. It was inevitable that they would be invited to take over the afternoon shift on the national youth network Triple J. But even if it was inevitable it was still a huge moment.

When they started their radio show I was working at *Inpress* and volunteering at Melbourne public radio station Triple R (a bastion of community radio). I'd done many of what's known as a 'mid-dawn shift', which is what it says, from midnight to dawn. I was also occasionally filling in on Triple R's breakfast show when an already established Kate Langbroek was away (thanks to comedian Dave O'Neil for giving me this break, too), and I was contributing arts and visual arts reviews on Bruce Beresford's Thursday morning arts program, in line with some arts writing I had also been doing for *The Age*.

Radio seemed to be everything that print was not. Sure, you had to prepare in advance, but it was immediate, both in output and connection with the listener. That was a rush. Print, while exciting, took a lot longer to form (for me, anyway) and the result seemed more permanent, more concrete. Radio felt a little wild, a little reckless, a little dangerous. I've always been attracted to that. And you could play music too – share your favourite sounds with listeners, take them on a journey with song, which is the best thing about music, either for yourself or for a group of people. At this point in my life, radio seemed like the greatest gig ever.

So when Merrick and Rosso asked me to provide a weekly entertainment report on their show (I guess they thought I was qualified, given all of the above) I jumped at it. I hadn't grown up with Triple J, it had only made it to Red Cliffs long after I'd moved away, but I was sure getting to know it now. The boys made me so welcome that I became part of their regular team (which included the divine Tom Williams, who was known as Tom, The Chippy From Manly, and had originally appeared on the show as a caller).

As part of the show, we'd travel the country, in one of the early radio stunts for which Merrick and Rosso became loved for, in a bus named 'The Love Bus', stopping at regional towns all over Australia. On these trips I learnt so much – about radio, about presenting in crowds (I was the one they'd throw to for vox pops), and about the addiction of live radio. It was a hoot!

From working on the Merrick & Rosso Show, I started doing my own mid-dawn shifts on Triple J, while holding down my print job too. Sometimes I wonder how I did it, working full days on no sleep, and partying whenever I wasn't working. The only reason I think I managed is because I was young and running on the exhilaration of it all.

Then Triple J offered me my own show on Saturday nights, taking over from the beautiful Rosie Beaton, who had established a radical new chart show called The Net 50, where people could do the most cutting edge of things and vote for their favourite song *online*. I know! Whodathunkit? Use the computer to vote? What sorcery! This was at a time when the internet was still dial-up and people were yelling at their mums to get off the phone so they could spend seven hours downloading porn, pixel after slow pixel ... so it really was quite novel.

I was charged with collating the votes, which were painfully printed line by line on a dot matrix printer, then counting them down on a Saturday night to a wide audience all over Australia. If you think the internet's cooked, try answering a Triple J phone on a Saturday night in the '90s. I don't think I've spoken to more truckies, farmers and kids off their nut at parties since. It speaks volumes of the reach that Triple J had, and still has in regional areas, and the breadth of people it attracts. We should never forget the vital role the station has in helping young people in these areas feel connected to the rest of the country. I wish I'd had something similar as a kid, because it would have meant everything to me.

It wasn't long until those Saturday nights morphed into various other jobs around the station, finally leading to a permanent gig hosting the lunch shift for five years. Then eventually, in my final year at Triple J, I hosted breakfast with Frenzal Rhomb musicians – the incredibly dry and hilarious Jason Whalley and the ever-energetic and life-affirming Lindsay McDougall, otherwise known as Jay and The Doctor. The team was rounded out by our super-producer Alicia Brown, whose knowledge of every follow-up and unsuccessful single from a one-hit wonder meant that I adored her instantly. It was a wild time.

One of the highlights of my time working at Triple J was their One Night Stand concert program, where small towns would bid for some of the biggest acts of the day to come to their town and play a concert. As someone who grew up in a country area, where one of the most exciting things to happen was the Big M girls arriving in town, something like this would have been right up my alley. I loved seeing a town embrace an idea, from the local school to the local shops and the local CWA, and then everyone from the local mayor to the local stray dogs turning up to get an idea of what the kids were up to. And the kids! Their beaming faces radiating pure joy was enough for me to know that this gig was a gift that would be remembered for a long time.

Country kids aren't outsiders, they just don't get the same chances to enjoy things that city kids take for granted because they're easy to get to. This was a magnificent subversion of the norm. I'll never forget the AWOL concert I participated in, in Burnie, Tasmania, a coastal industrial town an hour and a half from Launceston, where people opened their arms and hearts to us so wide that we ended up partying till all hours with the locals at a local dance studio, then riding bikes up and down hotel hallways to no recriminations. I've never felt so safe on a night out on the town. Burnie embraced our travelling musical tornado with gusto.

These events are testament to the role that Triple J has, which is more than just providing a voice for youth, it connects kids around the country with a shared voice, a shared narrative of songs and ideas. In a time when the online world has given us more options and less connection, I do feel this is so necessary. I don't listen to Triple J much anymore, because it's not for me. It's not meant to be for me. I am way too old and I should be uncomfortable listening at times because I'm not the demographic they're aiming at. Rusted-on Triple J listeners sometimes find this hard to grasp. I also don't need music to help me define who I am in the same way that I did when I was younger. But I don't doubt younger people still need it.

It becomes pretty obvious when you're too old for the Youth Network, and by the time I left, at the age of thirty-four, some around the building considered me to be positively geriatric.

It was time to go. I was being courted by a commercial network, Triple M, with an offer to work with my friend and talented, so-naturally-hilarious-it-hurts comic Pete Helliar in a breakfast radio gig in my hometown, which was too good to pass up. But I learnt an awful lot from my time at Triple J – I honed my music knowledge, I established myself in the Australian musical landscape on many levels, it opened many exciting doors, I made incredible friends and had a wild time doing it all. It was here I also met my darling and talented friend Zan Rowe, who I now co-host the podcast 'Bang On' with (still through the ABC). We started as broadcasting babies in Melbourne, and to find ourselves working together again at this stage in life, is a joy and a pleasure.

* * *

I started at Triple M in January 2008. Pete and I were sent in to replace an outgoing and long-serving, much-loved breakfast show. We knew it would be an uphill climb from the start but remained unfazed and prepared for it. We had jokes about the band Nickelback ready to go ...

We quickly realised we needed an anchor for the show, and Pete was friends with a comedy writer and brilliant radio presenter who he thought would be perfect for the gig. His name was Richard Marsland, someone who became not just a workmate but a dear friend too.

There was a lot more going on for Richard at that time than he ever spoke about. Even as recently as 2008, mental health was not something you discussed at work or even much in a private context. Richard absolutely never discussed his struggles with us and was always ready to work. I'm so thankful things have changed and that people are now becoming more comfortable opening up about their battles. I only wish this had been the case for Richard. I'm not sure if I was naive, but I genuinely didn't know at the time that something was deeply wrong, as he was a master at hiding it.

Our first year was tumultuous. Our ratings were flailing and we were struggling to juggle the commercial with the creative. By the end of the year we were feeling very uncertain about our jobs, the show and our future at Triple M. After the final show of the year, we had lunch at the pub next door to celebrate the fact that we'd made it through. Champagnes were drunk and everything seemed okay. Next year was a new year, a fresh start – all the cliches were thrown around. I'd had a few more than I should have and the ever thoughtful, gentlemanly Richard helped to bundle me into a cab. I will never forget the certainty with which he said to me that day, 'Goodbye, Myf.'

The day after, Richard committed suicide. He had so much life to live and give and he deserved to experience it. I'm still so deeply saddened for him and his family by what happened.

I wish I'd known more about mental health back then. It was absolutely never talked about, and it should have been. I've had my own struggles since, and because of the tragic, senseless loss of such a talented person who was loved so dearly by all who knew him, I know that it's important to be more honest about these things, to hide nothing. And for that, I thank Richard. Beautiful Richard. I wish he had known that it was okay to not be okay, that people would have listened, and we all would have dropped everything to help, if need be.

* * *

Radio has been the place where I've experienced some of the greatest highs and lows of my career. It's where

I've put all of myself in, because it's impossible not to. When you do a radio job you never clock on and off, it's relentless. You're always working and looking for content. It's an incredibly human medium. If you tried to put on an act in any way it would be exhausting. Listeners can hear through any kind of pretence. It's my great love and my great frustration, because it never feels like you will ever get it right. And that's the point. It's perfect in its imperfection because it's delivered by a human, not an algorithm.

* * *

The show with Pete limped along after Richard's death but we both knew the day was coming. By July 2009 it was over. But my radio career wasn't. Years later, I was happily living in London when Australian radio boss (and I mean that in the dual way, she became my boss but she is a BOSS – a font of ideas, a passion for radio and a true supporter of creativity) Meagan Loader approached me to return to Australia to help start up a radio station at the ABC. It would be called Double J (which was Triple J's original radio call sign) and was the next progression for listeners after Triple J. I'd been listening to BBC6 Radio in London, which was doing this very thing, and I was loving it. Even though I loved my London life (I had been living there for nearly two years, scraping by with varied jobs), this *really* was an offer too good to refuse. When else do you get to start a brand-new radio station?

It was a great honour to introduce the nation to the new station and play the very first song that would be broadcast, which I knew would be written down in history books. The song was so apt, chosen by the extremely thoughtful and considerate team behind the station, who knew the weight of such things. It was an honour to press play on a fellow Australian with a broad view on the world, Nick Cave and his Bad Seeds. The song was 'Get Ready For Love'. It will forever be the song that reminds me of this new, exciting chapter in my life and a joyous return to a format that I love so much and that has taught me so much, about others and about myself.

Spicks and Specks

(Barry Gibb)

10.

Captain Myf

Who knew a television show, other than *Countdown*, would become a huge part of my life. And Molly would appear on both!

The first night *Spicks and Specks* aired, way back in 2005, my mum called me afterwards and said, 'I hope you taped that [on VHS, remember those?], because it'll be good to have something to remember this experience by.' Little did Mum, or anyone else, know that the show would go on to become much loved and would still be on TV, nearly every night, on ABC's second channel, seventeen years later. Had I known this, I may have toned down a few of my outfits, wild hairstyles and makeup, which at the time seemed perfectly fun and normal. Now they seem a gorgeous time capsule of a young woman's willingness to give anything a go, not thinking any of it would be kept for posterity.

So how did it all come about? When I was working at Triple J, hosting the afternoon show, I got a last-minute call to audition for a TV show that the ABC were piloting. All I was told was that it was a music quiz show, and it would be hosted by Adam Hills, an Australian comedian who had spent a lot of his time working in the UK and Europe. Alan Brough, an actor, comedian and writer, would also be on it. Alan and I already knew each other – we had hit it off one afternoon at a mutual friend's party where we'd bonded over our love of music – so I was pretty chuffed that I'd see him again, this time in a work capacity. I had no idea that both these men would become such a huge and formative part of my life, and two of my best friends. I love them both dearly and thank whatever god she is who brought us together in such a serendipitous manner. Hillsy is a genuinely caring, clever and thoughtful soul, who deserves every bit of his wild international success (he's a big deal now in the UK, didn't you know?) and Alan is the gentlest of giants whose love and support I cherish every day.

I barely remember the actual audition (or maybe we filmed a pilot that day, it's all a blur), all I knew was that if it went well the show would be filmed in full a week later. I guess if I'd failed the producers may have had other options, but I got the gig and was filming the first episode the next week.

I'd watched the UK shows on which *Spicks and Specks* had taken inspiration from – there is a tradition of this type of quiz show in the UK – but practically all of them were hosted by men, and had team captains who were men. At the time I didn't realise my appointment as a team captain was going to set the show apart from others, but I'm grateful for it, because the goal is surely to make sure you leave the world a little better, and that means more diversity on TV too. I must at this point shout out to a few people who made huge inroads at that time at the ABC for hiring folk out of the box – and they are Courtney Gibson, Amanda Duthie and Paul Clarke, and later, Anthony Watt. Their vision and persistence, and seemingly deaf ears to criticism, meant we had a chance.

I was ready for this new challenge. I'd been working at Triple J for seven years at this point and *Spicks and Specks* was exactly the something I needed to spice up my life a bit, personally and creatively. Hosting shows on radio, including my long stint on the lunch shift – featuring a trashy lunchtime quiz, combining music knowledge and pop culture – was also the ideal precursor. I needed somewhere for my useless knowledge to be used. *Spicks and Specks* seemed to have been designed to be specifically relevant to my interests.

So back to that first show. I was a deer in headlights, obviously. I was desperately trying my best to navigate the immense feelings I had working on the set in the very same studio that *Countdown* was filmed in, all those years ago (this was overwhelming for someone who simply dreamt to be in the audience for *Countdown*, not being the subject of a show!), as well as looking out at a full camera crew and production, a live audience and thinking about people watching at home (Hi, Mum!). It was a lot to process. And then, weirdly, I remember it being on the tellie not much more than two weeks later.

Spicks and Specks first aired on 9 February 2005 with Cal Wilson, Kram, Dinah Lee and Ross Noble joining our teams. Dinah Lee and Ross Noble were on my team, Kram and Cal Wilson on Alan's. We started off as we wanted to go on, with humour, entertainment and joy at the show's heart. Alan's team won that first episode with thirteen and a half points. My team wasn't far behind with eleven points (not competitive much). There were so many highlights from that show, like choosing 'Musician or Serial Killer', but singing during the final section of the show was nerve-racking. I much prefer leaving that to our talented guests.

The second episode was, for me, an absolute disaster in terms of worrying what critics would think of me once it aired. Being the young thing from the youth radio station (although, at this stage I wasn't that young, I was thirty-one, which was *old* by women-on-television standards then), it was my job to know everything about the music that we played on the station. If you grew up in the '90s, grunge was a hugely influential musical movement that was spearheaded by Nirvana. 'Smells Like Teen Spirit' was considered the anthem for that generation. *I* was of that generation. However, on show two, I let my generation down.

When the guitar intro for 'Smells Like Teen Spirit' was played, all that was required of me was to say the title of the song. With the aforementioned lights, cameras, audiences and pressure, do you think I could think of the name of the BIGGEST SONG OF MY GENERATION? Nope! My brain froze. I was completely and utterly lost. Just between you and me, I'm terrible at remembering song titles that aren't in the chorus, hence I'm known for singing an entire song before I can remember the name. But even that wouldn't have helped me this time because the words 'Smells Like Teen Spirit' are not featured anywhere in the chorus.

My failure to name the song left me beyond mortified. I was sure my peers would think that I was a fraud, or they would never let me live it down. Probably both. In the real world, it would not have been a big deal at all but for me, who was trying to forge a life as a professional music journo and broadcaster, it was not-so-laughably tragic.

Fortunately, most people thought the whole thing was hilarious. They could relate. So many have had 'that' day at work, and this was mine. I knew I would never live it down, but I would also grow to love that it happened because it showed me that I was free to be as imperfect as I needed to be on the show. Embracing imperfections is liberating. I recommend it highly. This was my first tentative step towards achieving that.

Looking back, I do feel sad that I worried so much about what I had done (or not done) and what people would think. I used to get upset driving home when my team would lose again and again to the brilliant Alan Brough's team (Alan's knowledge is unstoppable, but I do have a competitive streak). Hilariously, people would often ask me if we ever cheated on the show, if the producers gave us answers. My response was always, surely the producers wouldn't let me lose as often as I did if that was the case?

One of the best things about the show was witnessing the rise of someone like the brilliant Hamish Blake, who knew next to nothing about music, but charmed the pants off everyone he met, including the audience who adored him. Of all the guests we've had on the show, I think Hamish has made the most appearances, just behind the hilarious Dave O'Neil, who will never not be funny. Dave is testament to the fact that authenticity and honesty shine through.

Sometimes, in the early days, I wished I had a comedic shtick to fall back on, so that I could hide behind some jokes when I felt vulnerable or scared. But the older I get the more I realise how lucky I have been to be completely myself on a television show where being myself was accepted and celebrated. It's a rare job that allows you that, in any field.

The show gradually became a household name. We were on screens at a time when people were still mostly single screening (not too many tablets or social media then) and we made forty-one episodes that first year. Forty-one! That's nearly one episode a week for an entire year. In current TV terms, where a show is lucky to get six parts in a series, that number of episodes is positively bonkers. We were young, we were cheap, we were keen, we were having a ball. It didn't feel like work.

Sure, the first few episodes were a little loose, and so they should have been. No TV show's first episodes should be perfect. They need time to grow and evolve, and become whatever it is they are. Thankfully, 2005 was a time without the social media of today so we had the space to find our feet. I'm sure people at home were probably thinking, 'Who's this bunch of amateurs in my lounge room every Wednesday night?' and I wouldn't disagree. But this bunch of amateurs was having a lot of fun, and week after week people cottoned on to this and started watching and enjoying with us. We weren't perfect but there were a lot of laughs and a lot of heart, and we had the chance to develop on that without being hung out to dry and mercilessly criticised on social media, which too many shows have to contend with today.

I bemoan the fact that these simpler times have gone, especially when it comes to the creativity of television. If the negative axe falls online and enough people loudly decide something's not great, it's very hard to turn that sentiment around. In days of old, Terry at home would have said to himself, 'Get that bunch of wankers off my ABC', and while he may have had a point (I deny no one the right to call me a wanker), Terry's views probably wouldn't be printed as news the next day in the local rag, and people wouldn't pile on or just assume that everyone agrees with Terry. I should point out that I am talking Terry, not Kerry, here. Kerry Packer *could* pick up the phone and pull a show off air immediately, which he did in 1992 while watching Channel Nine's *Australia's Naughtiest Home Videos* with Doug Mulray.

All things creative need to breathe and, thankfully, we were given plenty of time to breathe, grow, mess up and perfect, without the constant glare of judgement. I'm not saying that TV should be judgement free, but I do believe that social media terrifies bosses, which has a trickle-down effect on what gets made. That instant judgement also makes it much harder for new people to deal with the barrage of criticism that putting yourself out there invariably invites. I struggle with it, and I'm already in a position of privilege as a white middle-class woman, so how hard must it be for anyone young and full of ideas to cope? I worry we are losing some brilliant shows, performers and entertainment moments because we are all too quick to criticise.

Luckily for us at *Spicks and Specks*, Terry never wrote a letter or spoke to anyone other than his TV screen (although he may have left a voicemail at the ABC) and we would go on to film for seven years. And in those years *Spicks and Specks* challenged the idea that the people appearing on the show had to be popular to appeal to a broad audience. We often did the opposite and instead showcased a huge variety of performers who were brilliant at their game, but not necessarily broadly known. It worked, incredibly well. From composers, singers, rockers, pop stars, to country stars and opera dames, the show offered a smorgasbord of musical talent and gave them an opportunity to broaden the minds of the viewing audience too. I also loved how it would sit older, established artists next to young up-and-comers, giving exposure to both when it's so needed. Life is full of challenges, careers go up and down, and while many artists have enjoyed being at the height of their game, maintaining a career as an artist in this country is a rollercoaster. One day you can be on every show in the country, and in ten years, the complete opposite. If anyone thinks choosing the arts as a career is an easy ride, then they're completely deluded. Add a pandemic into the mix and it's an even more precarious choice.

I am really proud of how *Spicks and Specks* showed the diversity of creativity in this country, and did not elevate one type over the other. Where else on mainstream, prime-time Australian TV would you see the glorious conductor Richard Gill (Vale, Richard!) sharing his knowledge of classical music and blowing us all away with his hilarious stories? Until *Spicks and Specks*, there probably wasn't a place for Australians to get to know him in such a real way. Richard subsequently became a much-loved and adored member of our *Spicks and Specks* extended family and I hope that, in a way, in a musical way, the show was always challenging people to look beyond their own boundaries, outside of their circle, to find a bit more joy and inspiration in the world.

People often ask me who my favourite guest was, and I never know how to answer. There were so many shows, so many people, and it all happened so quickly at the time. For me, it wasn't the big, international names who appeared on the show who had me quivering in my boots. It was the artists who I had grown up watching on television when I was a young girl and who had now settled into a comfortable middle age. Those I idolised. So many women, such as Renée Geyer, Chrissy Amphlett, Marcia Hines, Sharon O'Neill, Jane Clifton and Deb

Conway, came on not realising the impact they'd had on me as a young impressionable girl, and they didn't disappoint when I met them in real life.

When I told the always inappropriate Uncanny X-Men rocker Brian Mannix that I was excited to be sitting next to him because I adored him when I was young and had a poster of him on my wall, I was met with the hilariously inappropriate response, 'Well, I'm so excited. I'm glad I wore stretch jeans today!'

So much of what happened on the show probably wouldn't get through to the keeper now. It's truly a time capsule. I've never laughed harder than the day Frank Woodley, whose mastery of physical comedy is unsurpassed in this country, was charged with recreating a 1975 British clip in which Australian singer Little Nell (Nell Campbell) became famous for a wardrobe malfunction because she inadvertently exposed her breasts doing 'the swim' dance manoeuvre in her strapless swimsuit. Frank, in a faithful recreation, wore the same style swimsuit, did the moves all while mimicking pulling up the swimsuit as the trooper Nell did at the time. However, Frank also managed to expose much more than just his man boobs, all the while pretending nothing at all was amiss. Let's just say we all had a ball that night. IN OUR EYES.

These moments of pure, hilarious chaos made the show. Like the night my team, featuring New Zealand comedian Rhys Darby and Australian singer Pete Murray, bet that we would get naked if we won. Why? No idea now, other than I hadn't had many wins and it wasn't looking likely to ever happen. But who wouldn't want to get nude with a couple of fine fellas (gosh, this is all sounding very *Don's Party* circa 1973, isn't it? Keys in bowls, anyone?). Suffice to say, miraculously our team won and I ended up under our desk doing exactly what was promised. This was a huge achievement for someone like me, who was usually hung up about how I looked, often not thinking I was funny compared to the comedians, yet there I was, part of a moment of pure joy and hilarity that could never have been scripted.

It was an honour and a privilege to make *Spicks and Specks* the first time around. By the time it wound up in 2012 we'd done over 250 shows. At the time it felt right to end. We felt we'd told all of our stories, and as with anything that's going well, you always want to go out on top. We'd taken the show around the country as well, performing it live, using members of the audience as our guests and interspersing the show with comedy, singing, dancing, all performed by us. I'd never done any theatre (aside from high school) and here I was, eventually performing to over 60,000 people all up, on some of the most prestigious stages around the country. I caught myself asking, 'Who even am I?' as I pinched myself.

Having the opportunity to perform for two weeks, two shows a night, with every show sold out at the Enmore Theatre in Sydney, was something out of my wildest dreams. I'd only ever fantasised I'd be like Baby in the film *Dirty Dancing*, who gets picked to star on the stage much to the amazement of everyone. I never thought that would or could be me in real life. And yet there I was, being lifted by the gentle giant Alan, in what is Baby's signature move during our own rendition of the song 'Time of My Life'. This Baby was well and truly not in the corner anymore.

Five years later we'd do the live tour all over again, but this time it was a farewell tour as we said goodbye to the show. It was an even bigger production, if you think five sold-out Hordern Pavilions are a good measure, along with an audience of our then prime minister, Julia Gillard, and this time me singing and dancing Beyoncé's iconic 'Single Ladies' dressed in latex for our opening number. The show was so huge it was completely unreal. Sadly, now, with time passing, and the fact that my stage music career hasn't exactly kicked off after this (apologies to Beyoncé, what was I even thinking?), this now feels as though it happened to another person. Another fabulous person nonetheless. But I'm so thankful I had the opportunity to do it.

In those stage shows I not only got to tour with Adam and Alan, but also with my brother Kit, who was the musical director for the live show, and two other dear friends, Gus Agars and Stevie Hesketh, and our tour manager, Georgia Chadwick. It was like a travelling family. We had our own tour language, shared jokes, raucous poor behaviour, and we worked hard, played hard and laughed harder. I am fortunate to have experienced what it might be like to be in a band at the time you're on top of the world, without having to be in a band. I got to live out my fantasy for a time. Those seven years were pure magic.

But never say never in TV and, after reunion shows and a new series with Ella Hooper and Adam Richard as team captains and Josh Earl as host, the original team is back together again. Adam, Alan and I were offered the opportunity to return and do *Spicks and Specks* all over again (first in a limited run and now ongoing). We all said yes! The boys have their own reasons for agreeing to return but, for me, it came down to this: in this business, you do some jobs that are difficult and disliked by viewers, and some that fill you with joy. If you get one that fills you with joy, and you get to work with wonderful people while you're doing it, do it at any opportunity. I'd missed working with my buddies, so the decision was simple for me. I'm humbled that people still care and think of the show fondly, and that they still watch. It's simply nice to work on a show that is truly loved by people. That's the rarest of gems in this industry.

Also, if I'd received royalties for all the repeat screenings of the show (which I didn't), I would probably be in the Bahamas by now. So there's that ...

So *Spicks and Specks* lives on, and so does my connection with the Bee Gees (not just because of the name Redcliffe). Whether it is the Bee Gees' original or the TV version by the Dissociatives (Daniel Johns and Paul Mac) I can't not smile when I hear the song!

Theme from
A Country Practice

(Mike Perjanik)

11.

Frankly, my dear, I wish I didn't give a damn

Dear Diary,
Australian television's night of nights, the Logies,
was on last night. It was screened on Channel
9, which Mum doesn't usually let me watch. We
only have two TV stations in Red Cliffs where I live –
the ABC and Channel 9 – so I don't know some
of the people, but everyone is drinking champagne
and they all look so pleased to be famous and
fabulous.

I'd like to go to the Logies one day. There's no event
like it in our town, Red Cliffs. Unless you count our

*footy club's Pie Night where old men make speeches
about ball-handling skills that go on so long that white
spit forms around the corners of their dry mouths, and
then we all eat pies at the end.*

*When I grow up I want to go to the Logies. I want
to be just like TV personality Jeanne Little. She looks
like a hoot. She even wore a dress made out of garbage
bags.*

*If I went to the Logies I would perform the theme
from A Country Practice on piano. It's such a
grouse and emotional song, and I've learnt most of
it (well, just the start anyway, but that's the most
important part). A Country Practice is my favourite
TV show. I love that it's set in a small town just
like mine. In the performance I could channel all
the emotion into it that I felt when I watched one
of the main characters, Molly, die and her husband
Brendan screamed out, 'Mollllllyyyyyyyyyyyy,
NOOOOOOOO!' and then the screen went black
and my brother Kit was pointing and laughing at me
saying, 'Miffy's crying,' so no one would notice that
he was crying too.*

*Imagine if I met Molly or Brendan one day. I would
cry. I love them both so much.*

From little Myf's diary, 1985

If I could have told my twelve-year-old self, who dreamt of embedding herself in the cast of *A Country Practice*, that the Logies would be in my future she'd be screaming around the lounge room in front of our massive, brown faux woodgrain-covered Rank Arena TV, screaming, 'Nooooo way. You're joshing me. Don't josh.'

I am not joshing! I made it to Australian television's night of nights, the Logies. If you're from elsewhere that word probably sounds like something a little unsavoury, and you'd be half right. The Logies are a bit like the Australian Emmys, or the BAFTAs, with a few international celebs thrown in who usually have no idea what they're doing there – I'm looking at you Chris Noth, aka Mr Big from *Sex and the City*. I sidled up to the bemused American and offered an electrifying conversation starter of 'Are you having a nice time?', which resulted in him pulling a face like a screwed-up napkin. Clearly he was wondering if the payoff for attending this weird event in a far-flung country was worth the appearance fee and a cheeky holiday to the Great Barrier Reef.

I am not even joshing that at my first Logies I presented an award. As I stood on that stage I was more nervous than I'd been when I first held hands with a boy at a Saturday afternoon screening of *The NeverEnding Story*. I looked out into the crowd and saw local TV identities. Legends Bert and Patti Newton were on one side of the room, Molly

Meldrum on the other. So many faces from my youth, which I'd previously only seen from quite a long way away in the corner of a tiny box (as I mentioned earlier, Mum never let me get too close to the tellie because I'd ruin my eyes) or in a magazine. My fantasy world had come alive. It was terrifying and exhilarating all at once. I covered my nerves up by likening my dress to an oversized disco ball (referencing Jeanne Little's garbage bag dress) and pressed on. I then spent the night trying desperately not to get drunk on white wine, but obviously did because I have hazy memories of gate-crashing a Channel 7 after-party and toppling over on the dancefloor while doing the Nutbush in front of the head of Channel 7's news department. Can't imagine why I've never been offered a job at Channel 7 since ...

At the time, it was hard to see the Logies purely as a professional work function. The thought of being there in the flesh was still just too much! No surprises though, that I slept through my alarm the next day, missing my breakfast radio shift on Triple J. I woke to seventy-four missed calls from my workmates.

Fortunately, they saw the funny side, and I didn't get the sack.

At subsequent Logies, I put all my efforts into having a good time and trying to charm the pants off people I loved while also making sure I set multiple alarms for the next morning.

Then, the bad year happened. This was the rough year when I had left Triple J to work at Triple M with Pete Helliar. I loved working with Pete and he had boundless energy and optimism for the job, something he applies to all of his work, but I don't think I was quite as suited to the realities of commercial radio. The 4 am wake-ups were torturous. I was exhausted and stressed. Looking back now I realise I was also deeply depressed following Richard's death. I had little energy or happiness to share, which is not a good place to be when you have three hours of breakfast radio to fill with energy and humour. When you are depressed, finding the spark to entertain is hard. I was struggling personally and professionally and unsure what to do.

At this point, clothes were my last concern. I was treading water and couldn't be bothered thinking about how I looked. So, when I was invited to the Logies that year I farmed out the thing that I had the least bit of energy for, the clothes.

For once I enlisted a stylist and a dressmaker so my outfit was sorted. This is what I thought all the professional TV people did to ensure they looked their best. I'd been winging it on my own up until this point and, sadly, I didn't get the memo that this was also the year that fashion critics were sharpening their knives. Dissecting the outfits of those on a red carpet was on its way to becoming a blood sport. I like a giggle and have chuckled in both awe and envy at some of the outfits Céline Dion has worn over the years, but Australia's night of nights is not the Oscars and not everyone can look like Nicole Kidman on a red carpet. I am not six foot four but I thought I looked good! In my defence, it was the 2000s, the decade that fashion forgot when it came up with appallingly low hipster jeans matched with g-strings. I didn't wear them!

That year *Spicks and Specks* was nominated in the Most Popular Light Entertainment Program category, which is always a magnificent thing for everyone who works so hard on a show. It is even more magnificent when you win, but we didn't (for trivia buffs, *Rove* took the Logie that year). I didn't get drunk because I was determined to do my best and wake up at 4 am for work. Our ratings on the Triple M radio show still weren't going great and I didn't want the year to get any worse.

So, the next day, with crusty eyes and a handbag full of stories about celebs I now can't remember the names of, I arrived at the studio, opened the newspapers, and there it was. A picture of me, photographed from an unfortunate angle, showing off my double chins to their best advantage, wearing a dress that, under lights, looked even brighter than the turquoise eye shadow worn by Boy George in the '80s. The fashion critics didn't take to my little one-armed turquoise number. They felt my feeble attempt at a fun and festive peacock had failed and said it looked like the truly glamorous birds at the Logies, who towered right over me, had taken a very glamorous turd-shaped Swarovski crystal dump on my shoulder. The story went on to say the public got to vote on best and worst dressed, and the results would be published the next day.

It must have been a slow news day because the next day on the front of the biggest local paper in Melbourne (the *Herald Sun*) there was a photo of me stretched to make my five-foot self look of equal height next to the best dressed of the evening, ex-model, glamazon and daughter-in-law of the owner of the paper, Sarah Murdoch.

She looked stunning in an expensive dress. No guesses as to who was voted by the *Herald Sun* readership as the worst dressed? Little ol' moi.

Look, there are way worse things that can happen, but at the time I genuinely thought I was being laughed at by the entire town. The worst thing is, I'd never cared too much about clothes but this front-page business left me feeling ashamed. There were plenty of other things I probably could have been shamed for (like actual naughty behaviour) but this seemed unfair. My dad gave me the best advice at the time. He said, 'Today's news, tomorrow's fish and chip wrapping' – I still use that wisdom to this day, but after that year the shine was definitely off going to the Logies.

At this time in my life, when everything else was going down the gurgler, I felt pretty low. I was being compared to women who did this sort of stuff for a living and it made me question my judgement, my appearance and my body. I compared myself to people who had the time, money and help to prepare and I found myself wanting. That was not good.

I am on the tellie, I put myself out there and this kind of thing comes with the job, so I have to be cool with it. But I was so not cool with it that year. I didn't hate the dress (by the 2000s fashion standards, it wasn't that bad) and I was an easy target. Low-hanging fruit.

I was embarrassed but I shouldn't have been.

In the '90s when I developed my style (if you can call it that), most of us took pride in not caring what others thought. It was an era of anti-fashion, anti-judgement, and no waxing (that made life easier and cheaper, I must say, although shower drains were much hairier). The 2000s were a very different era. But the problem was, I hadn't noticed. I was still walking around with my '90s attitude. Wear whatever, Riot grrrl, fuck the patriarchy etc. What's disappointing was that for the next five years or so that unflattering photo of me in a dress that everyone laughed at was dragged out whenever the Logies rolled around, and I became known for the funny dress, rather than what I did or said on a show where I was proud that I had to use my brain.

Every year, the little shame flame would be reignited. I dreaded the Logies. I still dread red carpets of any kind and hide from them if I can. I'm sure that there are many public-facing women who have shrivelled from public life because of a shaming of some sort, and there are much worse types of shaming than being told your dress is bad. Women everywhere are shamed over their politics, their outspokenness, weight (gain or loss, everything's fair game), attractiveness, age, or just because they might refuse to play the performative game by being nice or appropriate and give a side eye instead. Hell, news outlets and websites thrive on telling women how they don't measure up daily. We know it's wrong to look at this. But we still look. I look. I click through. It's a vicious cycle.

Working at a commercial radio station, it's par for the course that your personal life becomes public. Radio producers clasp their hands together to try and work out how to make anything in your life a narrative they can involve the listener in. Fair enough, it's their job. Most do it well. I kept the bad dress narrative going by inviting the person from the newspaper who'd sunk their boot in the hardest on to the show and I burnt the dress in front of her. There was no satisfaction from burning the dress. It felt wasteful. I felt stupid. The designer and the stylist were deeply embarrassed – and, all in all, it was just an experience in the bitchiness of the media that I wish I'd dealt with better and cared less about. At least for the people who are following behind me.

So, hear this, twelve-year-old me who desperately wanted to go to the Logies. You will get to go. (Stop screaming and running around in circles in the lounge room.) You will have fun perving at people you never thought you'd see in the flesh – they'll be a lot older and shorter than you ever imagined (why is everyone in TV, except for Alan Brough and Matt Preston, really, really short?). You will get to touch some of your idols (even if it was just a dare to lightly touch Bert Newton's bum as you walked past him at the after-party; sorry, Bert, but at least it wasn't a lock of hair or anything, I'm not that weird). But going to the Logies changed you; don't let it.

That Logies experience took much of the joy out of working in TV for me because I realised I was living a life that was public in ways I hadn't expected. It was only a dress, but the criticism hit me hard at the time – mainly for other reasons. It made me sad later that I didn't stand up for myself and back myself, as I should have. I would have previously and would now. It made me sad that I actually cared so much about what people thought. I let the bullies win. Bullies always move on, there's always a new target, but the one thing I learnt, and this stuck in my heart the hardest, was to be kinder about other people's choices. I learnt to think from the perspective of people who might not do things the way I'd do them.

I learnt to have empathy for those who are easy targets, no matter how easy it is to laugh sometimes from the sidelines. I learnt not to judge anyone as harshly or as quickly as I might have. I learnt to celebrate those who take greater risks than I was capable of. At the time, I missed that in myself. I made it a goal to get that back. And I did.

A year later I went back to the Logies wearing a fabulous dress accessorised with a dash of fuck you. I didn't win any prizes, but I felt okay and could smile in the face of the judgey folk. A year later *Spicks and Specks* won a Logie. I'd promised Adam Hills that I wouldn't say anything if we won (because that never happens, so really there was nothing to worry about), but unfortunately, because I didn't think we'd win and I no longer had an early morning radio job, I'd taken advantage of the cheap white wine. So when we did win I ran up on stage and, slightly tipsy, just couldn't resist having a word at the end of Adam's much better prepared and well thought out speech.

I stuffed it all up by mumbling something about the show being a success because we were allowed to be honest and true to who we were, 'no bullshit'. Way to go, classy lady.

But I really did give fewer shits. And that felt better than a million-dollar dress.

Of course, my mum was not impressed with the swearing. And a mother's shaming is far harsher than a public shaming.

Oh, and I did finally meet Brendan from *A Country Practice*. His name's Shane Withington and he's on the soap *Home and Away* now, so he's still on the tellie and he's lovely. Weirdly enough, the night I won my one and only Logie, the bloke who played Brendan made friends with my partner and they were having so much fun that my partner wasn't even in the room when our award was announced.

Boyfriends come and go, but my ability to play the theme to *A Country Practice* on piano remains. And I felt vindicated knowing that famed rock star Iggy Pop recently recounted that when he was living in Switzerland with David Bowie, Bowie was obsessed with *A Country Practice* too. So much so he made Iggy watch the show constantly. When Bowie toured Australia in the '80s he insisted on meeting the animal mascot of the show, Fatso the Wombat.

Sadly, Fatso was unavailable, too busy being Fatso and eating and sleeping, I suspect, so Bowie had to make do with meeting Shane Withington. The very same man who I met at the Logies! I am forever comforted by the fact that one of the greatest musicians in the world loved what I loved as a twelve-year-old and there's every chance that he also plonked out the theme from *A Country Practice* once or twice on his trusty piano. Just like me.

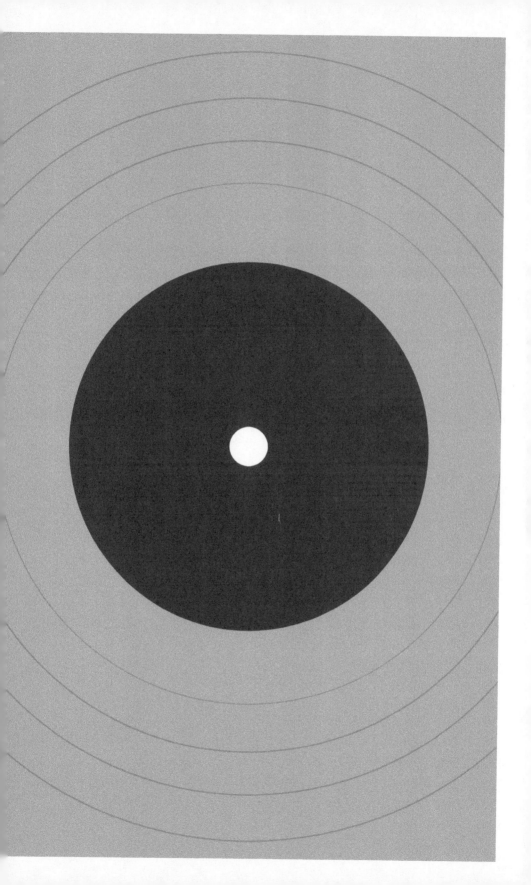

12.

'I'll see you down the highway'

There are a million songs out there about love. But how do you write about a big love, a long love, a real love, a problematic love, a rollercoaster love, a love that eventually ended? How do you put that into words? How do you do it justice? I'm not sure I can. For someone who always believed music could tap into every feeling, I struggled to find the song that captured all the feelings. Now, I'm not sure a song can. Life's too messy for all the details to work in a song. But I want to write this. Because the person who I shared all of these things with, who I once loved deeply, is no longer here.

Mike and I were casual acquaintances through the music scene in Melbourne. How it moved from that to something more is still a mystery to me. But I will be forever grateful for the day it happened. My life changed. His did too. And we took each other on a journey all over the world. Now Mike's not here to tell his side of the story. He'd probably hate this if he were. He loved a story, but one where he was the funny guy at the centre, making everyone laugh and, tragically, his story isn't fun anymore.

Now that he's gone, I am the keeper of all those memories we shared, and I want to let people know how special he was, how mostly wonderful our time spent together had been. Writing this is a little selfish, too, as I'll never get to say to him again, 'Remember when,' and laugh about how ridiculous and stupid we were. I want to remember, because I want the world to know the person I fell in love with, because if he was here and you met him, he'd charm the pants off you on his own terms, with no need for any kind of help from me. The world is a lesser place without Mike.

The magic between us happened on the day of the SLAM (Save Live Australian Music) rally in Melbourne, where thousands of Melburnian musicians and music lovers converged on the streets of the city and ended up at Parliament House to protest the effect of new liquor licensing laws that were crippling live music venues in the city. A gazillion Melburnians (mostly wearing black, what else?) took our pale night-time skin into the daytime sun and onto the streets to protest. The feeling that day was one of unity. Regardless of the type of music you were into, we were all buoyed by the knowledge that we knew, collectively, that what made the city of Melbourne great was that you could see whatever you liked, any time of the week, at venues all over Melbourne. The music scene was the late-night heartbeat of our city. It was imperative to stop any kind of barriers to make that pulse diminish. It's also a lot of people's livelihood, which we wanted to save. The protest led to a reckoning of the value of music to a city's identity.

Mike was a drummer in a band that was much loved both here and overseas. When he performed, he was a beautiful, intuitive drummer who was mesmerising to watch. He also sang his own music, the content of which was perhaps more revealing of the person he was than the hilarious and clever one portrayed publicly. There was a darkness. A sadness, a vulnerability. It was hard to spot initially when you met public Mike, but for private Mike it was bubbling away under the surface.

It was pretty obvious to others at the SLAM rally that we couldn't stay out of each other's orbit. Texting furiously at our wittiest for the next few days, Mike then asked me out on a date. An actual date. Not sure about you, but I've not been asked on many dates. Actually, none before this. I was nervous. He asked me to a movie. I can't remember what the movie was, but I know that when I met him at a bar across the road from the cinema he was wearing what I'd later learn was his snappiest jacket. He was making an effort. He also didn't take it off the whole night because it was hiding the patches of nervous sweat that had formed on his shirt underneath. It was a relief to know that one of the coolest, funniest people I knew was nervous too.

The night was long. We laughed, we giggled, he came back to my place and we kept things going. We drank too much because we were both brimming with nerves and excitement, and I fell asleep on him, apparently mid-sentence. I seem to have an off switch that works without prompting when I've had enough. This didn't deter him from wanting to see me again.

At the time we met, Mike was living at his sister Ali's place. I came to love her too. His relationship with his family was one of the things that attracted me to him. He was adored by them, and they were close, which made me feel safe. Someone so loved had to be a lovely person. He was. From that moment, we were inseparable. He stayed over so often he then moved into my house and we made plans to travel together. His band was about to tour overseas and I was in-between jobs, so we could test the waters of our relationship and start an adventure.

When you travel with someone you see all sides of them, and we travelled well. He made me feel as though I was looking at the world through new eyes. Together, we felt invincible.

Our first destination was the white-washed Spanish hillside town of Vejer de la Frontera, where we swanned around eating and drinking all the delicious things that just taste so much better when you're on holidays and fresh in love. We then flew to the UK, where Mike would be playing a festival called All Tomorrow's Parties. Located in a budget family holiday resort called Butlin's in Minehead, this festival was a lovingly curated one, where an artist or an act of great repute would curate a weekend of their favourite music. Normally the headline act at Butlin's when the families were there was a cheesy, faded UK star more suited to pantomime performances, but this festival flipped the place, and the idea of what a festival could be, on its head. Everyone from Sonic Youth, the Yeah Yeah Yeahs to filmmaker Jim Jarmusch and *Simpsons* creator Matt Groening had a hand in curating individual festivals. This was all the brainchild of two wonderful people who would later become friends of mine, UK promoters Barry Hogan and his then partner, Australian Deborah Kee Higgins. It was an extraordinary, eclectic festival where fans and performers would mingle happily, and get their minds blown as much by a huge headliner as an obscure noise act. There was not another festival like it, and given the financial peril of putting something like it on, there will, sadly, probably be nothing like it ever again. This was our first outing as a couple, with me meeting the others in Mike's band. They were kind enough to welcome me with open arms too.

We partied well together, Mike and I. We both wanted people around us to be as sparkling as we hoped we were. We loved fun and we made sure others had fun too.

There was a downside to this though. Occasionally Mike would suffer debilitating anxiety attacks the next day, where he thought he was going to die. It had happened before me, and I suspect it continued to happen after we broke up. He would use alcohol to level out again, which makes perfect sense, until it becomes a dangerously vicious cycle, a coping mechanism that was near impossible to break in a world where you're touring, performing and travelling constantly. The show must go on, and does go on, whatever it takes.

But mostly we were having a ball. We even survived a flight through mountain ranges in Mexico in a plane that was so old it had ashtrays in the doors. The pilot opened the doors as we were pummelling down the runway in order 'to let some cool air in', only slamming them shut as the wheels lifted off the tarmac. He then proceeded to put one of those silver shades across the windscreen to block the sun and proceeded to text all and sundry on his Nokia 3310. *Through a treacherous mountain range!*

We survived that flight. We found happiness in the most ridiculous of situations. We were good together. We felt full. We were in love. For a very long time.

Mike asked me to marry him when we were living in London. We'd moved over there when I was at a loose end, career wise. We had called time on *Spicks and Specks* after seven years, and I wanted to start fresh somewhere else. I suspect Mike wanted to make more inroads into Europe, this time with his solo songs. Thanks to one of my grandfathers, I could get an ancestry visa for the UK so London seemed like the right choice. Mike could tour with his band from there. Pre-pandemic, we thought we could live anywhere. As long as you could jump on a plane to get home, you'd be fine, right? How things have changed.

The afternoon we got engaged we had been wandering around the Tate Modern, and then dined at a restaurant in Soho. I didn't think anything was up as Mike was usually in charge of choosing the restaurants. He loved food, which was incongruous with his tall, slight frame. The restaurant was reminiscent of what old Soho would have been like, before gentrification. It was extremely cosy (the sharing of an armrest on a flight kind of cosy) and served simple, hearty food. There, over a bottle of wine, he brought out two wedding bands he'd had made by a jeweller friend of ours and asked me to marry him. I said yes. I'd never thought I'd be the type to get married; I love a wedding but had never envisaged my own, but I couldn't imagine a life without him in it at that point. We called our families and made plans to get married in London at a registry office. It was to be no fuss; an acknowledgement of us being a team for life. We could party with friends and family later.

Juggling our lives in London wasn't always easy. With Mike touring, me trying to get a foot in the door with erratic work, and trying to understand English bureaucracy made things a little complicated. It's much harder to start fresh in a new country when you're nearing forty than it is when you're twenty. So when Meagan Loader approached me about that dream job to help launch Double J, I deliberated for a while but knew that going home was the right choice. This was a once in a lifetime opportunity. Our wedding plans were put on ice.

Unbeknown to us, the process of returning to Australia with animals (our cats, Terry and Steve) meant we would have to wait twelve months before they could even fly back to Australia and go through the quarantine process. It was heartbreaking to find out our cats had to stay while the requisite time passed post vaccinations. Mike stayed with them in London. I relocated to Sydney.

I suspect this was the beginning of the unravelling.

It was hard being separated from all of them. The new job was wonderful and challenging, but I knew I wasn't mentally ready to leave London and had left quite a lot of myself there. Leaving Mike there, in particular, I felt my heart was broken in all the ways it could possibly be.

By the time Mike joined me back in Australia, cracks had started to appear in our tight and usually pretty fun ship. We weren't being as kind to each other, we were more easily frustrated, life just felt more real, harder. There wasn't as much to look forward to and I think we might have resented each other for that. It was as if our vision of each other and us together as a couple had changed. This was it, our real life, far from the sparkling fun of London and Europe. This was real. This was hard. Something had shifted. Neither of us was particularly happy.

I won't go into the specifics, because it hardly matters now, but sometimes relationships end because they should. Relationships are hard work, and you have to want to do the work to keep them alive. By the end, neither of us wanted to. The finish was, as all great loves that end are: a little ugly, nasty, petty. It was a painful severing of ties, friendships, dreams and shared narratives. It's the stuff you're not proud of afterwards but know that it was what you did to survive.

Sadly, I would never speak to Mike again in person, although I never thought this would be the case. I guess I always assumed that one day we'd be able to look past what had happened and be the friends that we should be, given what we'd experienced together. We had too much fun together, not to. In his last few years we communicated only through email, but fortunately the tone grew lighter and lighter as time passed. The last few emails we shared, spurred on by the unfortunate and sad shared news that one of our cats, Terry, had died, saw us also discuss the issue of some missing records that were still being sourced from storage units. We both laughed about the fact that, even though they were missing and that the blame looked to be firmly on me, he knew I would never secretly hoard his Bob Dylan records, even out of spite. My love for Bob was not on par with Mike's. I don't think I've ever put a Bob Dylan record on by choice in my life. It was nice to finally find some neutral common ground again and to laugh. We were taking small steps towards an inevitable friendship down the track. His final email to me, sent in the year he died, read 'For what it's worth and you don't have to reply but I'm sorry for the way things turned out. I really do hope you're happy.' I never replied. I wish I had.

Mike died during the long lockdown of 2020. I watched his funeral on Zoom. It was horrible. There was no collective grieving, no laughter and no celebrating of his life. Just me on a couch with a friend, watching through a screen. It was a send-off of songs and stories from friends who loved him, but an event that shouldn't be happening. The dissonance was real. I was asked to make a video sharing my stories of Mike. It was lovely of Mike's family to offer me that opportunity, given their loyalties. It was a beautiful ceremony in the strangest of times and I think I'm still recovering from the shock of it all.

Mike told me a fabulous story once and I tried to share this one with his friends. Of all the tours he did, he loved the experience of supporting Neil Young on his Australian tour. It had been a few weeks and, as yet, Mike hadn't had the opportunity to say hello to the legend.

When his moment finally came, and Neil was to honour him with his presence, Mike had just returned from the toilet and was in a bit of a rush. He hadn't washed his hands. Neil proceeded to extend his hand to greet him and commend him on his drumming, which left Mike with a split-second decision to make. The hand loomed large. Do you miss an opportunity to shake Neil Young's hand? Mike always took great pleasure in retelling this story and building the anticipation. What he chose to do, I'll leave to your imagination, but he would also repeat Neil's poignant parting words to him that day. 'I'll see you down the highway.'

Those words meant so much more on the day of Mike's funeral. 'I'll see you down the highway.'

Whatever highway Mike is on, I know he's making the most of it, making new friends.

As we all know from personal experience, music offers the greatest of all keys to our emotions. That is why this chapter has no song as a step-off point. After Mike died, I hadn't been inclined to put on a record. For two years during the pandemic and lockdowns and Mike's death, I didn't listen to music at all. I couldn't. I faced my own silence. I'm only just starting to feel ready to open that door again.

Mike died of an aneurysm brought on by bouts of heavy drinking – as a result of trying to cope with serious mental health issues. He was forty-two. His greatest fear that propelled his anxiety came true. That's all I know. I can't think about it too much, ever. But what I do know is that we'll never get to be the friends we would have been eventually, and never get to laugh about those life-affirming and altering times we shared. I will cherish them always. The world is a lesser place without Mike. He had so much more to offer.

And for what it's worth Mike, I'm sorry too.

Africa

(David Paich and Jeffrey Porcaro)

13.

Not in Kansas anymore, Toto!

One would hardly think that the brassy flute sound played on the keys of Toto's song 'Africa' would stir something deep within me at one of the most pivotal and transformative times of my life. When the song came out back in 1982, I loved it, but I wasn't even ten years old then and if you were any older, like my brothers, you weren't allowed to love this song publicly. Yes, it is a finely crafted ditty about the love of a continent (congrats on that kind of subject matter getting to number one around the world, Toto), but it was by no means cool. At all. Too smooth, with a staunch whiff of aged cheese about it; its lack of sharp edges was considered by the tastemakers of the time to be the embodiment of saccharine, soft elevator music that was infiltrating contemporary pop. If you loved Toto, it seemed you might also wear white linen, drink a sweet spatlese lexia white wine and ... (to be honest, at my age now this sounds totally acceptable, even fun). Back then, if you thought you knew a thing or two about music, Toto were 'The Enemy'. They were like daytime soaps to Shakespeare. The level of disdain was high.

It took a long time for me to shed the embarrassment of my love of this song. This happened around the time I decided there was no such thing as a guilty pleasure, and I could embrace every unwrinkled, glossy edge of this dorky, ultra-earnest synth fiesta.

After nearly four weeks of being isolated deep in the African jungle with a bunch of folk I mostly only knew beforehand because of their 'celebrity' status but had got to know intimately since we were all lumped together for Season 6 of the reality TV show *I'm A Celebrity ... Get Me Out Of Here!*, we were all woken up in our camp with this song blaring over the sound speakers, which were usually reserved for producers telling us off for not wearing our microphones around camp. A feeling of warmth, comfort and pure joy enveloped me tightly. As a Byron Bay wellness coach would say, 'I felt held.' It had been a long, challenging month living in the jungle in South Africa, with no contact with the outside world, no stimulation of books, screens or phones, and no food, and I'd unbelievably made it almost to the end.

It was quite a journey (for want of a better reality TV term) to get to South Africa and make it through relatively unscathed, which might go some distance to explaining why hearing 'Africa' was such a moment for me. On my first day, I was regretting my choice as I teetered outside the door of a helicopter hovering among the mountains of Kruger National Park in South Africa, with only a bungee jump cord tied to my legs, about to become the first woman in South Africa to bungee jump out of a helicopter. Clearly, hell had frozen over or I'd lost my mind, or maybe both.

Why did I say yes to doing a show that was known for making celebs (and all of us on the show used that term lightly) do things they didn't want to do, all for your entertainment at home? Many people were wondering this, since I'd mostly chosen non-commercial projects in my professional life. I'm what you might call a public broadcaster staple, an ABC kind of gal. In the same way some people believe there should be standards with the type of music you listen to, people who profess to 'not have a TV at home' or 'only watch the ABC' also decided that me being involved in reality TV was a shocking development in their understanding of me as a person. These type of people make their views on your choices very well known. It's best to avoid them and go forth and enjoy your life however you darn well please. And, stuff those people, listen to whatever makes you happy.

There were a number of contributing factors that led to me signing up. I've always been a huge fan of reality TV. Way back since the days of the first *Big Brother*, where I would sit at home alone on a Friday night in the mid-2000s watching the live stream from the prison house full of cameras. I was utterly astounded that unscripted, uncensored, regular folk could be shown on TV. This radical new format was raw and honest, and to me seemed the perfect vehicle to observe and understand ourselves. Sure, the format has now veered into the worlds of people who are so far from real that they're almost a fantasy projection of human behaviour and appearance, and much of the drama is scripted, but no amount of plastic surgery, money and thinking you can buck the system can save these participants from still showing us parts of who they really are. Contestants can say all they like about 'editing' (which, of course, can be easily manipulated), but if you're an absolute horror show in person who emotionally manipulates others, I'm pretty sure the viewer will see that. And that's why I *still* love the format. Humans aren't the greatest at pretending to be who they aren't. And scriptwriters couldn't write some of the stuff that these mere humans say and do. In fact, the drama that many bring to reality TV would be howled down in a writer's room for being unbelievable in the real world. But it happens.

Channel Ten had approached me a few times to be involved in *I'm A Celeb* and, while flattered, I always said no. I didn't want to expose myself, warts and all, to the world at the time. I was scared that if I showed my whole self, I wouldn't be accepted, that I'd be somewhat of a letdown. What if people found the real me rather dull? Not funny enough, not smart enough, ugly in my own skin. Getting older has led me to caring a bucketload less about what people think of me, but these things still niggle. I'd like to think I've got a thicker skin, but that's not quite true. I'm just less worried about the opinion of strangers. Back when I was first asked, no amount of money could have lured me to Africa. Mostly because of the creepy crawlies, slithering things and prospect of being forced to eat impala anus as one of the challenges.

So what changed? Why had I gone from 'That's not for me' to 'Oh yes, that's for me'? A surprising amount, to be honest.

One of the things that spurred me to go to Africa was that I had been told my daily ABC radio job, a national music and arts show on ABC Local radio, which I had poured my heart and soul into for two years, would not be renewed. My contract was cancelled. I was blindsided, lost and baffled, my ego bruised and my heart heavy, and

I was also wondering how I was going to pay the mortgage. It was a case of knowing I had little to lose – and it was certainly not a job, because I no longer had one.

Most people go on *I'm A Celeb* because they're at some sort of a crossroads in their life. They do it to make money, to reinvigorate a career, or to change direction. I did it for all three reasons. I also saw it as an opportunity to do something so totally out of my ballpark, where I would potentially get to have fun with a whole bunch of people I didn't yet know, in a beautiful country I hadn't yet visited.

It remains one of the best things I've ever done.

People have sometimes mocked celebs who go on these kinds of shows, especially those who might have been out of the limelight for some time and are perhaps struggling to make a living. The nastiness of this kind of journalism, which assumes that fame is the only thing that people might want and once you've had it you can't go back to living a normal life, is irresponsible at best. For most of us who work in the entertainment business, we're all just one job loss away from pivoting into something else entirely through necessity. So when you next lol at a story of someone who was once on *Home and Away* and is now working in real estate, and you sense that they're being mocked for it, take a step back. Think about someone who might have had a big role back in the day, who you haven't seen for a decade. How are they paying their rent now?

The entertainment biz in Australia is small, and jobs are hotly contested. It's lucrative at times, but it's swings and roundabouts. Unless you forge your own path, you basically get gigs or lose them because someone in charge makes the decision to hire you because they like you, or the audience does. A successful career is about having talent with a dose of pot luck.

So there I was. Jobless, a little heartbroken, ashamed that I'd been sacked from something I was really proud of, so in the spirit of the great orators of our time, I said, 'Fuck it, I'm in!' Fear of heights, snakes, creepy crawlies, be damned.

And that's how I found myself teetering above Kruger National Park, my legs tied to a rope connected to the undercarriage of the helicopter, about to bungee jump into a ravine. This was only day one of the whole experience. At this moment I certainly questioned the life choices that had led me to this point.

The day of filming had started with me blindfolded, high up in the hills, being led around a house that we learnt was a secret 1960s James Bondesque pad, perched atop a mountain that at some time was used for 'secret government business'. I later discovered this house high up in the hills was where government ministers took their mistresses for some dangerous liaisons. It had only recently been made accessible by road. So running away really wasn't an option for me unless I was some sort of ultra-marathon runner. That and the fact the wildlife out there would probably enjoy taking a bite out of me, attracted by the scent of my tears and fear, kept me on track.

In order to get through just day one, I'd downed a whole bunch of beta blockers that I'd had prescribed for my recently diagnosed anxiety, which had developed while I was treading water in my radio job. Thank goodness for them. I don't recommend a pill for things but, frankly, I was so anxious when Julia Morris and Dr Chris Brown told me of my fate, I was certain a heart attack was incoming. I fell to the ground. Terrified. Thing is though, I'd signed up and I truly did want to raise money for my charity – a gorgeous organisation that looks after the pets of the homeless, as well as underprivileged and domestic violence sufferers in their time of need. Everyone, no matter what their circumstances, deserves the love and hope that pets give us. They're called Pets of the Homeless if you're interested; donate if you can. I wanted to raise awareness for this organisation and do them proud.

I can't tell you the gut-wrenching horror and fear that comes with doing something you had absolutely no desire to do in your life *ever*. I'm not a bucket list kinda gal (unless it involves buckets for tasting and spitting wine in various different countries, now that's a challenge I can embrace) and I can't think of anything worse than adrenaline-based activities. Yes, I did jump out of a plane way back in the '90s to see what it was like, but I also wore dark, dark burgundy lipstick in the '90s and that doesn't make it right. I hated jumping out of a plane so much. From the minute I was attached to the guy wearing the parachute, I knew I was in for a bad time. After we landed everyone else felt as though they'd been to a Rainbow Serpent rave all weekend, while I had to have an extended lie-down on the ground to recover, gripping on blades of grass like they were life ropes and trying not to vomit. To me, adrenaline junkies are just people who don't have enough going on in their lives. Who has the time or the inclination to make life scarier than it already is? And yet, here I was, again, about to bungee jump out of a helicopter. Prior to this, I hadn't even been in a helicopter.

Two things were running through my mind at this moment, which led me to the inevitable. One, I came all this way to South Africa to jump in headfirst because I had nothing to lose, right? Two, I suspect the people who are rigging up this bonkers apparatus and frankly nuts idea are probably the best in the country at it, so I'm probably not going to die today, right? I also didn't want to be the first one to say those famous words 'I'm A Celebrity, Get Me Out Of Here!' which would get me out of the task, but mean less food for the team at camp, who I hadn't even got to know yet. I didn't want them to think I was a lightweight.

Words can't describe the feeling when I took the dive and the contents of my stomach pressed towards my brain. As my eyeballs tried valiantly to grasp onto my pink inner lids and *not* fall out, there I was falling, out of a helicopter, on a bungee rope. The only thing I could do to halt the terror of my current reality was to close my eyes. It helped, marginally, until the bounce of the bungee jump as I reached the end of the rope and I was flipped straight back up in the air like a sad spin on a Coca-Cola yo-yo. And then I was left just hanging there, underneath a flying helicopter, trussed up like a Christmas ham. I didn't think it could get worse, but it did. Way worse.

What you didn't see on the TV was that the hanging part went on forever. The flat ground necessary for the helicopter to deposit me on land was around ten kilometres away. So there I was, just hanging there, upside down, like a leg of jamon in a Spanish tapas bar, flying under a helicopter, contemplating my life choices. Miked up with a GoPro on my head, I remember mumbling something about feeling like I was on drugs (which clearly didn't go to air – but adrenaline will do that for you) and when my boots started to feel like they were slipping I thought I was a goner. As I watched the ground swish past underneath me, it's true that when you are faced with what feels like imminent death, everything does slow down. The only problem was, my death wasn't coming that day. I just had to endure this painfully slow form of torture to get through day one.

I've gotta say though, the sense of achievement I gained from doing something as ridiculous as this was strangely satisfying. Would I do it again? Nope. For all those who suggest jumping straight in to cure a phobia – like jumping out of a plane to overcome a fear of heights – you're wrong. Doing this absurd exercise did not cure my crippling fear of heights or disdain for adrenaline-based activities. Give me a blanket on the couch and Netflix any day over that ridiculousness.

Trauma bonds people, so it's no surprise that I bonded immediately with some of my new jungle buddies. Nothing like a bit of post-traumatic stress to bring disparate people together. There was the beautiful Tom Williams, best known for his shirtless win on *Dancing with the Stars* (who, as I mentioned earlier, I knew from when we worked on radio together with Merrick and Rosso, back in the day) who was suffering a little more than me on day one. He thought it would be funny to jump out of the helicopter rather than fall, as instructed by our serious facilitators. His bold choice meant he landed funny and bounced awkwardly, which messed his back up significantly. The bruising around his legs that appeared the next day was pretty horrific too. Understandably, he vomited on landing from the pain. Also not shown.

I bonded immediately with the eternally positive Energizer Bunny that is chef Miguel Maestre, with whom I shared a section of the camp where there were only two beds. We nabbed those straight away, knowing it would mean we were a little removed from what became known as the highly populated slum area, and it meant a little more peaceful sleep too. We older folks, we're wise, and we'll maim for a more peaceful spot.

The first night is a blur. Shaken, sunburnt, overwhelmed with meeting too many people and dealing with the reality of the situation, which was that we were sleeping outside, all alone in the jungle, surrounded by more cameras than a staged Kim Kardashian paparazzi shot. It was *a lot*. The exhaustion I felt that first night was next level. Almost delirium. As we were sent to bed and the lights went out, I do remember the slight horror of hearing the monkeys fighting, shitting and pissing on the canvas that was over our heads to protect us from rain, and the horrific, blood-curdling yell of the baboons living not far off in the distance. If you've never heard a big male baboon yell, you haven't lived. It's like a really huge terrifying man yelling out at random intervals, the sound so alarming it feels as if you might be brutally murdered if you came face to face with one. The sound our big baboon was making was like he was yelling a name. Someone in the camp, I think it was comedian and one-time *Married at First Sight*'s Ryan

Gallagher, deciphered the yell as 'BROB'. So that's what we called the big boss baboon. By the end of my time in the jungle, the sound of Brob was comforting. But for those first few nights, it was utterly terrifying. It's now the name of our WhatsApp group where we still chat, two years down the track, bitching about how easy the subsequent versions of the show have it (it's now filmed in Australia due to Covid) compared to our experience.

Our camp was really in the jungle. Base camp, where production happened, was about a ten-minute walk away. So there was always a slight possibility of a leopard making its way to the camp. Highly unlikely, but when you shut your eyes of a night, being the next meal for a big cat isn't something you want to think about too much. And let's not forget the tiny scorpions that can sting you to death, the cobras that kill with just a spit of their venom, and the black mamba snakes that were apparently everywhere.

When people go on *I'm A Celeb*, they talk about how transformative the experience is, and I'm a card-carrying member of the support for this show and the experience you get out of it. As much as I hated it at times, it pushes you in ways you never thought possible, and bonds you in a very real way with people you probably wouldn't have spent any time with otherwise. But what they don't tell you is the difficulty of the minutiae of the everyday. The depressing food and the lack of it. What makes one second on camera of someone stirring a pot is sometimes the one highlight of the day, given we were all so starving due to excessive rationing. The hunger is real. You're also detoxing from everything you're used to eating outside – food, booze, sugar – and from fun, life, dreams, communication, distraction, life. There is none of that. What's left is stories from your campmates, which are mostly pretty great. But after a few weeks, the stories start to run dry, and the mundanity of every day starts to take its toll.

The food on the show is utterly awful. Sure, there is meat for the meat-eaters and vegetables for those of us who don't like eating the beast, but it's meat like you've never seen or heard of before, chosen specifically to challenge every part of your understanding of what's edible – and what's okay to eat. Here you are in the jungle surrounded by some of the most extraordinary creatures in the world, and then you're eating them or watching celeb chef Miguel try and work out a way to make the gamiest, stinkiest of meat taste vaguely edible, cooking it all in one pan with no seasoning or sauce. From impala to nyala, they all had great names, and sounded tempting, but it was hard to get your head around eating some of the gorgeous animals that were living right beside us. Also, I'm pretty sure the producers picked the weird meat to be extra confronting on purpose. The night a small grey pigeon carcass was sent down the rope in the dilly bag that delivered our food was the night that nearly broke some. When glorious Rhonda Burchmore, star of stage, musicals and screen, and far too dignified and glamorous to be eating such muck, discovered the bullet hole in the breast of the bird, the mood changed. Watching an entire camp sucking sullenly from the bones to get the most measly morsel of meat to feel vaguely full was like watching last drinks at an over-forties nightclub as people scrambled to latch on to someone, anyone, who might fill a hole on that particular night.

I tried to remember that the whole point of the show was to make our time in there difficult, because that makes for great TV. Of course the food wasn't good. Rice and beans sounds quite edible in theory, but if the rice they give you is South African wild rice that doesn't soften even when boiled to a pulp, and the beans so hard even after extended cooking the baboons wouldn't eat the leftovers after we put them out for them (true story), nothing can help you. Most of us responded to this food in different ways. A: no probs, can eat anything and nothing touches the sides (see footballers Daisy Thomas and Billy Brownless – there's something about people who play footy that means they can put absolutely anything down their gullets, not sure why) or B: a bloated stomach the size of a sail on the Sydney Opera House, and subsequently blocked up like the *Ever Given* trapped in the Suez Canal – which was most of us women in camp. Some of us literally didn't shit for days. Me included. Some five days, some seven, one ten. That can't be healthy. We were a camp full of beautiful souls, but the food had us reduced to our base level, blowing off like bugles and high fiving when someone finally deposited something in the long drop. There was nowhere to hide. When you're in the jungle camp, all shame is thrown out the window pretty quickly. Which is a good thing.

What wasn't liberating about the experience was showering. I'm of an age where I have to stop caring about what people think of my body (even though, sadly, I still worry) but the idea of not showering nude and vaguely rubbing and washing about your bits while wearing a bathing suit is kinda weird. There's a reason why we wash in the nude. To get clean. But when you shower in the jungle for the first time and see cameras moving around to capture you at your most exposed, it is a tad confronting. So, for at least a week, my bathers stayed on. After that week, all bets were off. In front of a camera. I mean who am I? Pamela Anderson? I dunno who's got the tapes of all of us showering, I'm hoping they're deleted or burnt, but when you get to the point where you say who cares, knowing full well it'll never be shown anyway because it's too rude, and you bare all just to get clean, you know you've gone full *Apocalypse Now* bonkers. Most of us got there. I got there. In any other work place, exposing yourself would be illegal. On *I'm A Celeb*, it's a perfectly normal activity.

I also wasn't prepared for the toilets – I know my memories are purely food and daily ablutions thus far, I promise this will change – but when there are no distractions from daily life, these things are a *big deal*. We had a problem with the toilets. One drop was the short drop, for wee, the other, the long drop, for number twos. Both initially were cleared and cleaned by two people who will forever be legendary warriors in my eyes, *Love Island* alum Erin Barnett and comedian Dilruk Jayasinha. They took on the job of disposing of our effluent sludge on a daily basis, without hesitation. They are actual angels. I hadn't watched Erin's season of the reality show *Love Island* so I came to her career cold, but I can safely say, I have not met a more caring, thoughtful, and all round sweet yet resilient woman. If you watched Erin when she was tasked in a challenge to pamper our national treasure, the queen of showbiz Rhonda Burchmore, you would have seen the beauty deep within her. And Rhonda. The camp matriarch. The singer of songs and teacher of tap dance routines. A woman so deeply funny and entertaining to her core, which also houses a huge heart. To be in such company was an honour and a privilege.

I was surrounded by great women during this experience – content queen Tanya Hennessy, comedian Nikki Osborne and UK reality TV superstar Charlotte Crosby too. For eons, women have been told to see other women as competition, but my experience in the jungle was the absolute opposite. These women were not of my world or friendship group but they were supportive, funny and downright gutsy. I'm so thankful I got the opportunity to meet them all. And the boys too. I bonded immediately with gentle, thoughtful magician Cosentino when he entered the camp a week later, and had some of the best chats imagining the fun we'd have on the outside with legendary footballer Daisy Thomas.

I felt the same way about the hosts Chris Brown and Julia Morris. Their job, that they obviously enjoy, is a difficult one. They have to both encourage us and comfort us as they lead us into each challenge, with the full knowledge that they are also inflicting some of the worst things we'll ever do/eat/touch/see on us. Sometimes, it's our worst nightmare writ large. They're well aware that at times like this, when you're also hungry and scared, you're susceptible to feeling a little attacked and might not be in the best frame of mind to accept the worst challenge of your life with an open heart. They get it. But they also relish in it too. As I said, it's a fine, funny balance.

I quickly learnt that in order to survive the show it's best to just be a good sport and play along like the pantomime that it is. When you start taking things too seriously or personally, then you know it's time to go.

Julia and Chris do their job brilliantly. What you might not see when watching the show is that when they come into camp to announce who's up next for a crazy ridiculous trial that must be completed to earn food for the night, everyone in the camp of rag-tag folk, drenched in campfire smoke, with filthy clothes, gets a little googly eyed. It's as if our first crush has sat down next to us at school. Given our state, these two start to take on the appearance of angels. Stockholm Syndrome is where the captured fall in love with the captors, and we all utterly fell for them both. We'd also talk about how nice they smelt after they left camp, which was kinda weird, but boredom and a lack of fragranced soap will do that to you.

Also, you're so bored in there from having no distractions that by the end you're hoping you'll be picked for a challenge, regardless of how horrific it is, you'd rather that than endure another day of monotony in camp. Even eating a bull's penis (which is just as disgusting and chewy and sinewy as you can imagine, and yes, I ate one) seemed like a fun idea compared to yet another day sitting around in the camp when everyone's story bucket was starting to run dry.

Our only respite was the nearby waterfall, which was a quick walk into the jungle, where, with permission, we could swim on a daily basis. This is where we did the real talk, even though we were still mic'd up in the water. It was there we whinged and bitched, hoping the sound of the waterfall would mask it. It didn't, but they rarely showed any of the footage of us swimming, or bitching, which is a gift from the producer gods, really.

So much of what happened probably didn't end up on the show. I'm not sure, as I've only watched a few episodes and I think I'll keep my memories of the time as mine, without seeing them again through a screen. I don't want my experience to be changed by what I see. It's understandable that only a few things get through, as twenty-four hours a day leaves little room for more than one or two storylines. And, frankly, for most of the day we were so bored and boring, lying around camp with nothing to do, that it's probs good you don't get such an extensive insight into how boring celebs can be under such circumstances. Celebs really are just like everyone else, in that we're mostly pretty darn boring.

What else wasn't shown? The day we were given sausages in bread (and we all lost our collective minds – a smattering of tomato sauce was a revelation after weeks of no sauces or spices of flavour of any kind) only to have them smacked out of our hands by a person dressed in an animal suit, and then me, so keen to eat said sausage, picking it up off the ground, Rhonda giving it a wash under the tap and then me continuing to eat it. I was that desperate.

Also, not shown, as far as I know, a whole lot of us, desperate for something sweet, taking down another person in an animal suit for one measly piece of chocolate cake.

Funnily enough, they didn't show me screaming, 'Get me the fuck down NOW!' at the ground crew at one challenge where I had to ride a canoe off the side of one of South Africa's largest waterfalls (beyond terrifying for me who's scared of heights) and was left hanging over the huge drop.

I knew my time was coming to an end. We were down to the last seven of the campmates, and I was fraying at the edges. I never thought much about how long I'd be on the show. I really didn't have any idea if the public would vote for me, particularly as I was considered to be more of an ABC identity than a commercial TV staple. I was just thankful I lasted as long as I did. There was no way I was staying longer than the two who'd fallen for each other in camp (Charlotte and Ryan) because everyone loves a love story, and the others remaining in camp had far more star power than me. So that morning when Toto's 'Africa' was played through the loud speakers, I knew in my heart the writing was on the wall. And it was okay. I swayed my body with appreciation, sang the chorus with gusto and thanked whatever god she was for keeping me safe from leopards and for bringing me an opportunity that I will forever remember as truly life-changing. A month of isolation, I thought, would stand me in good stead for whatever the future could hold.

Little did I know that, on return, I was about to go into almost two years of isolation, when coronavirus made its way into our lives ... and after that, that little trip to the jungle where I did weird things for fun, seemed like the best holiday I had ever had.

Home

(James Newell Osterberg Jr)

14.

Home sweet home

The divorce rate is skyrocketing at the moment. I have no doubt the Covid lockdowns played a big part in this. When relationships aren't working and you simply cannot escape from one another, except to go for a walk within a five-kilometre radius, home life can become pretty grim.

I had my moments in the hall of mirrors during this time. I spent eighteen months in the same house on my own with my two cats, Steve and Merv, and my dog, Vyvyan (purchased as a Covid companion puppy – best thing I ever did). I watched all of the Netflix and Stan TV shows it was possible to binge, spent two birthdays in lockdown, and got to know all the folk in my local coffee shop on a first-name basis. Prior to lockdown, I would have told you I'd never cope with such a situation, but I did – we all did – and aside from a small minority of vocal anti-lockdown people, us Melbourne city folk did it all knowing it was for the greater good of the country, even though we often felt it wasn't really appreciated, or the difficulty of it wasn't understood.

Coming out of that time, I know I was brittle. I felt as though I'd disappeared into myself so far that I would not emerge like a gorgeous butterfly, but rather return like a shrivelled old prune. Thankfully, I'd faced myself, every single bit of myself, and I'd survived. I also had the support of Katrina, my friend of over twenty years, who lived within a five-kilometre radius. She encouraged me to get outside and be physical. She is a true gift.

As difficult as it was to live with the uncertainty of work and, conversely, the certainty of being in the same place every single farking day, I do believe that experience propelled me to make some decisions about my life that I may not have had the conviction to follow through with if I'd had the distractions of a regular, normal day-to-day existence.

During lockdown, I started to undertake a lot more DIY jobs around the house, like painting the kitchen and redoing the backyard, and I realised that these jobs gave me a sense of purpose and achievement at a time when everything else felt rather wobbly. I really enjoyed doing the work. It was a form of meditation.

So I started thinking about where I wanted to be in the next ten years; something I've never allowed myself to do, given my career can be so topsy-turvy. Until this point I thought it was impossible to plan. But I figured that, since I was nearing fifty years old, it might be okay to do something radical, and make plans for myself and have dreams that were all about me. I always thought I would end up with someone to share everything with, but I was damned if I was going to wait around for that to happen anymore. I was going to make my life the life I wanted to live on my own.

Bar a stint in London and a couple of periods living in Sydney, I'd lived in Brunswick for nearly twenty years. It was time to move on.

I started looking to live somewhere closer to nature. As an isolated country kid I couldn't wait to get to the big smoke and live cheek to jowl with others. But now I needed a break from the inner city, and that isolated country life didn't look so constraining.

I needed somewhere that would offer me refuge, in a place I wanted to be, I wanted to reconnect with my younger me, who loved living differently, and create a real home for myself. One that would not only provide refuge, but reflect something about me too.

Iggy Pop once wrote a song about everybody needing a home where no one can get at you or fuck with you (his gloriously literary words), and I reckon he was onto something. Funnily enough, that might have been one of the songs I would get up on stage to dance to (rather drunkenly) with a bunch of other people at the Big Day Out in Sydney in 2011, only to be herded off by a bouncer as I danced a little too close for comfort to the guitarist James Williamson. I had to shamefully apologise to him the next day as I was coincidently seated next to him on the plane back to Melbourne. But Iggy was right in his simplistic expression of our most basic need for shelter. Home needs to be more than just a place to sleep. It's a place of safety and should bring joy and comfort.

My prerequisites were clear. It was time to get back to nature. I wanted to be closer to a river. My Murray–Darling roots were calling – once a river moll, always a river moll, it seems.

I didn't end up on the Murray or Darling river, but I came close. The river near me, the Birrarung (Yarra) river, courses through the heart of Melbourne but begins up in north-east Victoria.

It wasn't just the natural world that was enticing me to look outside the city. Remember I grew up living in a tram and the mud-brick house that our family built and so I have always been obsessed with architecture and interesting dwellings. Like music, it's a lifelong passion that began with Mum and Dad's books on alternative housing from the '70s. My parents were hippies before their time, without ever presenting as such. Whenever I've travelled, most of my sightseeing involved the usual galleries and restaurants, but I'd also check out any significant mid-century buildings I could find. Mid-century modern, international-style architecture has a simplicity to it that seems deeply beautiful to me, the less-is-more style speaks to me of profoundly thoughtful and careful design, and a belief that a beautiful life doesn't have to be a busy life.

In Australia, there are two modernist architects who most people will know by name: Sydney's Harry Seidler and Melbourne's Robin Boyd. Both of these men challenged Australia's understanding of what good architecture was. Boyd, in particular, was known as a critic of Australian architecture as much as he was a creator. His book, *The Australian Ugliness*, critiqued the featurism of Australian suburbia. In the book he defines featurism as 'the subordination of the essential whole and the accentuation of selected separate features', and his homes promised the opposite of what was popular. He made elegant, simple homes that were designed for the Australian landscape, rather than simply plonked on top, as most houses were at that time. Boyd believed that good design should be available to all, not just those who could afford it. He was one of the drivers behind the Small Homes Service in the

1940s that offered architectural plans at the bargain price of around five quid through the local newspaper, *The Age*. I loved that anti-elitist sentiment and I've been fascinated by Boyd and his work for a long time.

So, there I was looking to make plans and make changes, when I saw a link in a Facebook group featuring mid-century houses for sale and renovation. It led me to a very early Robin Boyd–designed house for sale in a semi-rural area. My interest was piqued. Sure, it looked like it needed a lot of work and love, but the bones were definitely good. Boyd's hand was all over this little shack. It had a flat roof, angled windows and glorious local stonework in the fireplace. It was a simple and extremely rustic shack.

I can only imagine how controversial and radical such a design would have been in the local area at the time. People who lived in the area were used to weatherboard, federation-style homes, so this forward-thinking design must have seemed as if a spaceship had descended on the spot. I am pretty sure it would have been accompanied by some partying, as it was built for artists, so that would have added to the radical nature of the place.

I thought I'd go and have a look, given I've been slightly obsessed with real estate websites forever, and I love to go and stickybeak at mid-century joints. I never had any real intention of purchasing it.

But, as soon as I walked in, I knew I could make this humble home work for me (and of course, Steve, Merv and Vyvyan). It was located on a reasonably busy road and it needed a lot of work. Sure, I could live in it but in order to get it back to its original state, I'd have to roll the old sleeves up and dive into a project that I had absolutely no experience in at all. I've never restored a house! Who did I even think I was? I'm not sure, but I did know that I wanted to push myself far out of my comfort zone. I was ready for a new challenge, one that would upend my life in a new and interesting way, but also make my heart sing.

Perhaps the Covid lockdowns had changed the neural pathways in my brain because I obviously wasn't thinking when, after seeing the property once, for twenty minutes, and being told that offers were due in at 5 pm that day, I put in an offer. And it was accepted!

The house is a dream home for me in so many ways. It's a dream that it's a Boyd. And it's a dream that it's mine.

Most people will also tell me that I'm dreaming to think I have the skills to undertake such a huge project of restoration. But you know what? After those two years of lockdown and uncertainty I have the courage to do things I would never have done before, simply because I now know the value of making a life that is meaningful to me, outside of my work, and outside of other life markers, like marriage or children. I want to create a life for myself that I love, and that I'm proud of, and have something solid that is not at the whim of the entertainment business. I recognise the value of a home, as well as friendship and family, and want to create a space where others can enjoy it all with me, too.

The plan? It's to bring the Boyd back to its original condition. I have to remove the later extensions and take it back to its original state. My hope is that this shores up the house to survive many more years and offsets the ravages of time. I feel like a custodian of sorts – my job is to care for this building and share it with others so Boyd's legacy and desire to change the way we Australians think about architecture and our homes lives on.

I also plan to build an extension, one that is linked to the Boyd, reflects the Boyd, but does not leave an imprint on the Boyd. The Boyd will stand alone, in all its glory. It's a sensitive task that I'm leaving in the hands of a brilliant architect, who understands the importance of both conservation and liveability, and the difficulties of combining the two. My little shack deserves that.

Sure, I have to work even harder to find the cash to do it all, but now I have an aim, a plan and a dream, and it makes the work even sweeter. So cheers to doing the next fifty years as best I can with the same enthusiasm that I approached the last fifty! In my own home sweet home.

Zero Gravity

(Kate Miller-Heidke, Julian Hamilton
and Keir Nuttall)

15.

Kitsch, bonkers, greatness - the Eurovision experience

When I was a teenager, living in Sunraysia, we only had two television channels. One was a composite channel featuring stuff mostly from Channel 9 with some local content thrown in; the other was the ABC, which was the only channel my brothers and I were really allowed to watch in our house. My folks weren't fans of 'that commercial rubbish'. Secretly, I would lap up any of that commercial rubbish whenever I was home alone and could change the channel. Just before my final HSC exams I had one week free to study and I spent the whole week doing *some* study, but every afternoon I made sure I watched the daytime soap *Days of Our Lives* followed by a game show called *Press Your Luck*, then I would debrief on the phone with my friend Lucinda. This is what happens when you say no to me, it seems. I will do exactly the opposite, even if it's in my best interests not to.

I *was* allowed to watch *Neighbours*, which I was obsessed with back then, deeply desiring to be Kylie Minogue who married my heartthrob Jason Donovan (I can sing both parts of the Jason and Kylie duet 'Especially for You', don't you know?). Look, to be honest, at this point I would have been pretty happy to pat Bouncer the dog, or peer through the curtains onto Ramsay Street with Mrs Mangel.

When SBS was finally broadcast into the area in the late 1980s, it was a revelation. And, whoa, it was a lot for this innocent little country girl to take in. I've already discussed the Saturday night world movies, which, aside from *Dolly* magazine's 'Dolly Doctor' section or a stolen copy of someone's parents' *Joy of Sex*, which many of us have never recovered from and will never look at bearded men the same way (or can't stop looking at bearded men – maybe that's just me?) there weren't a lot of options for any kind of sex education. As if I was going to borrow a book from the local library or from the high school library. I'd have been laughed out of town ... So SBS World Movies it was.

I remember a few faves that I absolutely adored. One, *Betty Blue*, a tale of an absolutely gorgeous young woman, played by Béatrice Dalle, who is living with mental illness and who falls for a hot handyman/writer (how very French). They get it on and then it all inevitably turns to shit, to the point where the man must kill her because she's too much to deal with. Clearly, this is a hugely problematic film, however all I could see in it then was the 'hotness'. This film was so hot, I had to cut my hair in a similar fringed bob shape as Betty to cool down. Sadly, I did not look at all like Betty; I was more like a Lego lady than a sultry French babe, so no handymen were coming for me.

Another fave was *My Beautiful Laundrette*, a 1985 tale of two star-crossed lovers of a different kind – Omar, a young South London Pakistani man who opens a laundrette and falls for childhood friend and skinhead, Johnny, played by a young Daniel Day-Lewis. It's a film that deals with all the big topics like racism, homophobia and, of course, the cruelty of Thatcher's England and the unrest that came with it. This was the first time I'd seen any kind of same-sex relationship portrayed in a film. Also, hot. Prior to that my filmic experiences were mostly heterosexual, unless it was coded for those in the know, like the Village People movie.

SBS World Movies also introduced me to Pedro Almodóvar, whose filmic works I adore to this day. Watching the black comedy *Women on the Verge of a Nervous Breakdown* in my lounge room in Red Cliffs, in the late 1980s, showed me that women's stories could be all the things the male-driven narratives were – sexy, dramatic, funny, and also as bonkers and kitsch as those early James Bond films seemed to be, but smarter. Almodóvar elevated the kitsch and the feminine in a way I still love today.

Speaking of kitsch and bonkers and terrific, something else caught my eye on SBS that was relevant to my interests at the time – the Eurovision Song Contest. The musical performances in the competition initially reeled me in, but then it was as if I was witnessing the thing I loved the most, music performance, turned up even higher, more extreme than I thought possible. Eurovision was an eleven on the volume dial, which of course we know from the movie *This Is Spinal Tap* is a volume level that 'does' exist – where big dresses, big hair, big ballads, wind machines and special effects are the norm. What's not to love?

In Sunraysia in the late '80s a huge part of our community was made up of migrants from Italy, Greece and Turkey. Many families had moved to the area in the post-war migration boom, due to the similarities of climate and landscape. Where the soldier settlers failed due to inexperience, the migrant community thrived, and the place is all the better because of it. For these families, pre-internet, watching the Eurovision contest provided a link to friends and families they missed in their home countries. Eurovision was a beautiful global connector. I knew it was deeply loved by many families around me, and I loved it for this reason, too, *and* because it was dramatic and musically bonkers at the same time. I am not sure whether the creators of the contest realised, back in 1956, the way the show would draw people together, but it has gone from a radio broadcast to an almost global television event in just under seventy years. And it has launched some incredible talent. Sure, everyone knows ABBA had their start there, but the exposure didn't hurt Celine Dion, Julio Iglesias, Nana Mouskouri or ... Buck's Fizz, who won in 1981.

Fast forward many years and when long-time Australian Eurovision commentators Sam Pang and Julia Zemiro decided to hang up their boots (they weren't forced, they chose to – much to many people's understandable chagrin, because they were bloody hilarious), I got a phone call from Paul Clarke, my old boss from the early days of *Spicks and Specks*. He offered me the chance to go in to SBS Melbourne to audition for a role as a commentator. Just the year before I had sat on my couch in my PJs, at an ungodly hour of the morning, sobbing as Dami Im came an almost-impossible second place – impossible given Australia had only been in the competition a few years. No one could have ever dreamt of this happening so soon. Because of my radio work, I was also appointed as an Australian jury member. It was a huge honour to judge the songs, given 50 per cent of the votes come from the jury votes and 50 per cent from the public. Safe to say, I'm a huge fan.

That day, at the audition, I had the pleasure of meeting for the first time a comedian I knew of but had never worked with, Joel Creasey. I knew that Joan Rivers had taken Joel under her wing on a tour of America, and I knew that he was very funny. What I didn't know was that he'd become one of my best friends and my partner in Eurovision crimes. It was a match made in glitter heaven. In the audition we bounced off each other with ease, genuinely laughed at each other's jokes and our chemistry was spot-on. I later found out that Joel's heart is as big as his personality, and that's a rare thing in this business. It's not often you get to be paired with someone you not only like working with, but love personally, and I can safely say I also enjoy the holidays we have taken after Eurovision with Joel and his partner, the gorgeous Jack Stratton Smith, as much as our professional time together.

Despite all of this, our first year commentating was what you might call, politely, a debacle. We were in Ukraine, following the win by singer–songwriter Jamala, who beat out Our Dami's 'Sound of Silence' for the top spot. Joel and I were facing a lot of backlash around our appointment from the hardcore Eurovision fans. I totally get this. People like what they like and they don't like change, and after eight years in the gig, Sam and Julia were much loved. We knew we had a lot to prove on that first broadcast.

In Australia, there are two broadcasts of the competition. One is in the evening, which is not live, and uses our commentary from the live broadcast very early in the morning Australian time. This first screening is watched by die-hard Eurovision fans, the ones who know all the stats. This is the audience who would be most critical if we made mistakes.

We were truly up against it in our first live broadcast. Five minutes before we were supposed to air, the satellite line connecting us to Australia and the broadcast dropped out. When the unmistakeable intro music for Eurovision kicked in, not only were our lines not up and running, but we were also hearing our own voices in our headphones. Not sure if anyone's experienced this kind of delay in headphones when trying to talk, but it's happened once or twice to me in radio and it has the effect of making you slur your speech. You sound drunk, twisting with the words as they come out of your mouth and back at you in your head. It's the strangest experience. Joel and I struggled through as best we could, with our voices feeding back and others in master control talking to us while we were on air. It was a horrific way to kick off our new chapter.

Suffice to say, our first morning did not go down well and we were hit with a barrage of criticism online. Some of the Eurovision fans who were angry then are still angry at us now. They probably want to be doing the job themselves. But it got better! And we have been asked back every year since. Thankfully, seven years down the track, the ratings are better than ever so it seems we may have even won a few more fans over.

When you're at Eurovision, and deep in the bubble in the final week, there is just so much going on. I have learnt that it's easy to lose perspective and difficult to remember what people love about the competition. And that's the fact that it is completely bonkers. By day four of rehearsals, things all start to seem perfectly normal, even serious. Sometimes Joel and I have to take ourselves aside and remind ourselves that it is funny, that the woman performing is up a ladder, wearing a horse's head in a fake room scrawled all over with chalk. It is important to remember that for the viewer tuning in, it looks like chaos! Yet everything about the show is far from chaos. What you don't see is the performers who are finessing their three minutes on stage down to every single vocal note and shot for the camera – and they take their horse-mask lady up a ladder very, very seriously. It's meticulous. Everything is dependent on getting this moment right.

Joel and I, on the other hand, are trying to do a marathon. The three broadcasts of two semi-finals and a final are each usually around three to five hours long, and survival is about pacing yourself to still be your best self at the end. We also work during the day, filming around town and interviewing the artists backstage, which takes forever when you're waiting hours to get a chat with one of the faves. Many of these artists, who aren't really known outside of their Eurovision moment, seem to think it's okay in Eurovision week to be a diva of epic proportions. And why not? This really is their moment.

But being stuck backstage forever means everyone is lumped in together. Even the big names still have to get their own food from the usually very ordinary catering area. I may or may not have had a crush on one of the singers from Sweden one year (not that I want to objectify anyone, but this gentleman had me quivering in a way I thought was not possible in my older age), but I was quickly brought back down to earth watching him order a crappy sandwich from the bar and struggle to unpeel the plastic. Stars, they're just like us.

I've also learnt not to party too hard. The job is simply too gruelling. Sadly, this means we're usually stuck winding down at the hotels, which are often in the middle of nowhere. Unlike the Big Five – France, Germany, Italy, Spain and the United Kingdom, the countries who contribute the most to the European Broadcasting Union so they automatically go through to the final – who get to stay in the best hotels, we lower-class entrants seem to be put up in hotels in industrial areas. Unfortunately, at these joints, the only wine available late at night is never great; in Portugal it tasted like something secret agents could use to poison someone. Never drink the house wine if it's made by the house. One or two glasses had me with the worst hangover of my life. When we saw Jessica Mauboy taking a bottle to her room after the final night, we prayed for her safety.

Over the years I've had the privilege to watch our representatives perform: gorgeous young Isaiah Firebrace singing 'Don't Come Easy' on our first year as commentators in Ukraine (he was only seventeen at the time); the brilliant Jessica Mauboy performing 'We Got Love' in Portugal; crazy-talented Kate Miller-Heidke, who entranced the world with her voice and performance atop those tall bendy sticks singing 'Zero Gravity' in Israel; and the mesmerising Sheldon Riley singing 'Not the Same' in Italy. It's been a wild ride, for them and us. Sadly, the wonderful Montaigne wasn't able to attend and perform at Eurovision in 2021 because of all things Covid-19. It's disappointing that she didn't get to experience the full force of Eurovision, because there is no show quite like it. When it comes to the best of the best, in terms of lighting, staging and sheer number of people watching, this is it.

Joel and I truly adore the opportunity to front this sometimes glorious, and sometimes completely wild song competition *and* to be the far-too-supportive and embarrassing stage aunty and uncle to our acts. The fact that we also get to host *Australia Decides*, the Australian qualifier extravaganza on the Gold Coast each year, is just an added bonus. We're proud to be able to have something that we have done from the very beginning, that enhances Australia's involvement in the biggest song contest in the world.

So many people still ask me why Australia is in Eurovision when we're not in Europe, and I gently remind them that there are now quite a few countries in the competition that aren't in Europe (Israel, for one). Once they realise the huge connection Australia has with the competition because of our migrant communities, it's a no-brainer. As I mentioned, I grew up in a place where Eurovision was valued, not just as a song competition, but as a way for many in my community to connect with home – it is definitely not the joke that some would believe it is.

I'm proud to commentate this crazy exhibition of talent, theatricality and music and to get the balance right between jokes about the sheer wackiness of it all, while appreciating the serious musicality of it too. It takes extraordinary skill to write a great pop song or ballad, and for too long this has not been acknowledged by critics and the wider music community, who predominantly thought that pop music was the trashier, more feminine and therefore less-valued side to contemporary music. It also takes great skill to master a wind machine while wearing a great white frock and belting out a ballad, and this skill has not been given the respect that it deserves. I am proud that it is my job to make sure that, in the future, it is. So if you have never had the joy of watching Eurovision, hang up the mirror ball, gather your family and friends and frock up next year to immerse yourself in this must-watch experience. And to those who are already hooked, you know exactly why I hope to keep defying gravity and keep coming back.

Make the World Go Away

(Hank Cochran)

16.

On the shoulders of Maud and Margaret

My family are big on sport and music but they haven't been so big on family history, or delving too deep. Mum always said that her family didn't have any great stories, and Dad's side seemed fearful of uncovering things that they may not have been able to deal with or comprehend. That in itself hinted at big things, dark secrets. But I had no idea just how big or sad uncovering my own family history would get.

I never thought I was famous enough to be included in the list of people asked to participate in the television program *Who Do You Think You Are?*, the show that originated in the UK and digs deep into the subject's ancestry. It's one of my favourite shows on TV. While I'm not someone who wants to dwell in the past – sure, it's nice to visit, through music and art, but I've never been one to cloak myself in a warm, comforting blanket and cling to the music and memories of the past. To me, looking outward, to the future, is where I want to be. My past is safely behind me, done and dusted, and that's the way I like it most of the time. Frankly, while I have no regrets, I reckon if there had been camera phones when I was growing up, I'm not so sure I'd have the career I have today. I pity the tweens who have been documented within an inch of their lives, and I'm thankful that there are no photos of me taken that time a huge rainstorm hit the Meredith Music Festival, lightning almost struck the stage when the Dirty Three played (a religious experience for some of us), and soaked us all. Afterwards, I took most of my clothes off to dry and then went safely to sleep in a friend's car, only to wake in the broad daylight without anything covering me. As I'd slumbered thousands of punters would have walked past the vehicle to head back to the stage area. I hate to think what could have been captured and come back to haunt me later if everyone had an iPhone handy.

But I'll admit now, sometimes the past can teach us a lot.

Filming for the show took place in Melbourne during the world's longest lockdown. Making TV was considered an essential service, so being part of the show busted me out of home and my own company. If we stayed in our production bubble, which we did, and took our Melbourne rules with us (masks, no socialising with anyone outside the bubble, no shopping), we could still get things done. The crew all turned out to be fabulous, sensitive and caring.

The whole experience of filming the show was life-changing, as it gave me an opportunity to do something for my family that they would never seek out themselves, and it made me realise that looking back can help you appreciate more deeply what you've got.

However, I was not quite prepared for what would be discovered and the effect it would have on me.

On the show, I started by looking at my dad's side of the family. Mystery had always surrounded his lineage, as his mum, Ruby, was adopted. She never spoke of her adoption so, subsequently, neither did Dad. As far as I could tell there was a cloak of shame hanging over the whole thing. To be born out of wedlock at that time was seen by society as a source of great shame and many women were forced to adopt out their babies and then continue on with their lives as if nothing had happened.

The only information our family had about Grandma Ruby's adoption was that it was a 'handshake' adoption, apparently common at that time (the early 1900s), where a child was passed on to a family more capable of caring for them on the basis of a small note and a handshake. Ruby's brother, Albert, who arrived a few years later, was also passed on to the same family so they could grow up together. Yes, it seems unfathomable today to be able to pass children around so easily, but when you look back through Australian history it is perhaps no surprise that children's lives were considered so disposable. Lower socioeconomic families, single mothers, those with no power and no money were more likely to have to give up a child and then pretend the child had never been born. It utterly breaks my heart.

It turned out Ruby was born in the town of Mildura, twenty minutes up the road from Red Cliffs, where I'd spend the majority of my young life.

Unbeknownst to all of us Warhursts, my great-aunty, the daughter of Albert, was a huge Australian pop star in the 1960s. Her name was April Byron, formerly April Potts (Ruby and Albert's adopted surname). And she was an absolute boss babe who was living my dream life, long before I'd even been thought of.

I found out all about her, via a Zoom link, from her two magnificent daughters who I now can't wait to meet in real life, Cinderella and Candy. When I was presented with these two names the day before filming, I had absolutely no idea what to make of them. They felt a little

Disneyland and American, and very removed from me. What I didn't expect was to see two women who looked a little like me, all big smiles and teeth, smiling out from the computer screen and ready to tell me about their beautiful mum, who was sadly no longer alive to tell her own story.

April was sometimes referred to as Australia's Elizabeth Taylor, because of the way she looked. She had grown up in Adelaide and hotfooted it to Melbourne to sing for the masses as soon as she could, where she appeared on shows like *Bandstand* and *The Go!! Show*, performing with Johnny O'Keefe. Her first recording, 'Make the World Go Away' from 1964, was a suitably heart-wrenching '60s emotional ballad that was covered by many, including Elvis. It was a smash hit for her and April was the first woman to record with the Bee Gees on the single 'A Long Time Ago'/'He's a Thief'. She also toured extensively around the country with Johnny Farnham. From what Candy and Cindy told me, apparently April and Johnny Farnham were sweethearts for a long time. Had I known this when I was a teen in the '80s, and positively frothing over Johnny's 'You're the Voice' Driza-Bone/soft mullet/ big voice combo, I would have completely lost my mind.

In 1978, April moved to America on the promise of a huge film role that never eventuated, but she and her two daughters remained there, where she performed at acclaimed venues and recorded more singles with the Bee Gees that have never been released. There they are again!

I mean, what a story! What an amazing woman. And she was my great-aunt! I was pleased to learn from Candy and Cindy that there is currently a television script in development exploring their mum's life because, like many female pop stars of that time, her achievements were not acknowledged or documented. They've been forgotten by history. Telling April's story through a TV script will hopefully place her back into the spotlight where she deserves to be, with her life and career celebrated.

The one thing you know when watching shows like *Who Do You Think You Are?* is that quite often things will start well, with a good news story about a family, only to violently deflate the viewer, and the subject, with something difficult or dark in the next minute. This was absolutely true of my experience. In the space of a day I could go from the elation of knowing that there was another pop-obsessed woman in the family (this one with actual musical talent) and then head swiftly downhill to darkness.

That same day, a historian presented me with a newspaper article telling the dire tale of a young girl, Maud, aged seven, who had been 'interfered with' by men and boys. The men and boys weren't arrested though, instead tiny little seven-year-old Maud was imprisoned, and then for her 'crime' she was sent to the Abbotsford Convent – a religious enclave on the banks of the Yarra River. Maud's mum, a cleaner, was deemed to be unfit to parent her. She was also labelled a drunk by the nuns and was told she would never see her daughter again. I know all of this because the nuns at the Abbotsford Convent kept meticulous records, and every relevant detail of Maud's life was mapped out in cursive script in huge folders kept in storage for decades.

No one warns you of the feelings you experience when your eyes wander over many names and then recognise one of your own. It's as if the words explode from the page and take on a life, the life of that person you know or are related to.

From waking until bedtime, Maud's life at the convent was a nightmare. The nuns educated the children so they could be sent out as cheap labour to houses all over the state. From the first day, Maud was working as soon as she woke, learning how to clean, to cook, to dust, to wash clothes, with only two half-hours of free time a day. It was decreed that there would be no physical contact at all between the children or adults, no toys were ever given, and the girls were not allowed to talk to the other children, nor make friends. If they did have to speak to another child, they were told they must not do the same the next day. They were forced to isolate from each other. They had no voice, no autonomy, no hope, no life experiences, no references for a normal life. They were essentially enslaved into a life of servitude.

I can't tell you how many times I've been to the Collingwood Children's Farm, which is on land that was part of the convent, to wander the grounds on a gorgeous summer day, to eat a breakfast of locally grown produce from the garden, to marvel at the farm animals and the architecture. I had never known of its dark past, let alone my connection to it. I don't think I will ever look at the convent in the same light again. It's wonderful that the place has been taken over by arts and community organisations, but the trauma that Maud and thousands like her would have experienced there will forever overshadow any beauty I previously saw.

I found out, from more meticulously kept records, that from the age of around eleven, Maud was sent out to work for various families but was always returned. The reasons weren't listed – it might have been only a short-term service, or perhaps she was considered a little troublesome and sent back to the nuns, as if she were goods or chattels, or worse.

Within the constraints of a horrific system of enslavement, with no friends and no life experience outside the convent, Maud still managed to rattle the odd tree here and there. That gives me some joy. And hopefully gave her some too. There was a fire inside her, I can tell.

Maud was sent to a farm in Victoria at the age of seventeen and again returned to the convent a few months later. This time we know the reason. She was pregnant. It was recorded that Maud told the nuns the father was a 'simple man' who could not be accountable for his actions. However, once back in the relative safety of the convent, she revealed the truth. She had been raped by the farm owner. Her only safe escape was to blame someone else, probably to avoid being beaten or even killed by the real culprit. The nuns have written in their notes that they believed Maud was of good character and that they had no reason to think that she was lying.

So what to do when you're seventeen, pregnant, with no family and no friends? Maud was sent away to give birth and, according to more records, she tried to keep her child, holding on to her for an entire month (an extremely long time for a single mother in those days), but obviously it was simply impossible to go it alone, and after that month Maud relinquished her baby. Sadly, the whereabouts of that child are unknown.

Maud's life of servitude continued and she lived in Fitzroy in Melbourne, where she fell pregnant again, but this time she kept her daughter, who stayed by her side for the rest of her life. Maud then found herself in Mildura, where Ruby and Albert were born, and subsequently adopted out. Maud's story finally takes a happy turn when she married a man in a nearby town called Merbein and went on to have six more children with him. So my dad's mum Ruby's side of the family expanded, from two to ten, overnight. It was a lot to take in and I spent a lot of time crying as I unravelled the details of Maud's life. Thinking about how she lived with so little support as a child and teenager is difficult to comprehend. She must have had grit and determination to survive. From speaking to Maud's other descendants, it became clear that she carried the scars of her past as best she could. Her life was tough, but in the end she had family and a version of love that she had mustered up out of nothing. Given that her life and autonomy was cruelly taken away from her at the age of seven, I'm blown away by her resilience.

I often watch shows where tragedies of the past are revealed and wonder why people cry so easily, when they never knew that person. I get it now. For that small window of time, people you are related to but who you've never heard of come to life through words on a page, and it is an incredibly emotional and humbling experience to be able to acknowledge their lack of a voice and their struggle to survive.

The show gave me the greatest honour – I was able to tell my great-grandmother Maud's story when she had never been able to speak for herself.

What happened to Maud was only four generations ago. Knowing her story definitely makes me value what I have even more. Thanks to the fact she survived, I am here. I live a very unconventional and wonderful life where I can speak about the gains that have been made for women in this country. Even in simple terms, to have a mortgage in my own name (something that couldn't be done, even in the 1980s) would have been beyond my great-grandmother's wildest dreams. I've travelled the world meeting fabulous folk. All because of Maud's ability to survive in a system in which everything was stacked against her.

At the end of filming Maud's story, I had the honour of standing at her grave in a beachside suburb of Melbourne, where I acknowledged her trauma and quietly thanked her for all that she had done for me and my family. I promised to keep fighting for her and people like her. That moment was profoundly moving and I felt something shift in me. A letting go of others' expectations, perhaps. And the stirrings to share my own good fortune.

You'd think that was enough drama for one family. But there were more Warhurst revelations to come. The next part of my *Who Do You Think You Are?* experience had me trekking off to the very exotic locale of ... Bendigo, Victoria. Now, one might think that a trip an hour and a bit out of my home town of Melbourne wasn't exactly the most glamorous, but I'd been in a pandemic lockdown for so long I'd forgotten how to socialise properly or what travel even was. This was like an all-expenses-paid trip to a seven-star hotel in the Bahamas.

Bendigo was the home base for a thread of my family story that focused on my mum, Nancye's, side, and it turned out my great-great-great-grandfather Charlie was quite a reputable entertainer, who made his name performing around the thriving goldfields.

Charlie came from the UK to try his luck and created quite a name for himself as a satirist, putting the news of the day into song. While his life was not the grand success that I'm sure he hoped it would be, he did father a daughter, Margaret, whose own life foretold a type of feminism, albeit limited by strict societal constraints, that I can only admire.

Margaret chose not to follow in the footsteps of her father. Instead, she got married at a young age to a Scottish fella called John Carmichael and they proceeded to have ten kids. All I'd heard about Margaret was that she ran a wine shanty. I felt like this was a woman who knew how to run things and loved a good time. The opposite was probably the truth. Bearing ten kids is almost unfathomable today, especially for someone like me who has had none and struggles to get my own life and the life of a few ragtag animals together on a daily basis. To me, and the way I live now, getting through farm life with ten kids is enough of a success story. The fact that they purchased land in the Kerang area in Victoria – a rather scrubby, arid landscape – and were eventually considered a reasonably successful farming family is an even greater achievement. Sadly, I learnt that John died, leaving Margaret to farm and parent a family of ten kids. Impossible, at best.

Margaret did the best she could to save her family in this situation, and combined her interests with the next-door neighbour, who she quickly married. From what I can work out, this unification was more about supporting the family, a marriage of convenience of sorts, rather than some great romance. Again, there's a repeated pattern for women at this period in history. Like Maud, Margaret did her best with what she had, at a time when women had very little power or control over the family's assets or their future. But Margaret was smart. When news reached her that her new husband was about to blow most of their money on an impossible land deal, she had the foresight to purchase a multi-purpose hotel in her own name, in a tiny town with a name that evokes a glamorous holiday resort in Palm Springs rather than a dusty one-horse town en route to Swan Hill – Lake Charm.

Weirdly enough, I remember commenting about the town name when we passed through it a few days earlier, saying that it sounded so fabulous, promising something golden among the scrub, and I actually pointed to the exact colonial building on the roadside that I later found out was Margaret's pub, acknowledging what a great old building it was. The show's crew couldn't say a word of my connection to the place then, but I can't help feeling something pulled me towards noticing the building and commenting on the name. Funnily enough, I've always had a dream of doing up and running a destination '60s or '70s motel in the middle of nowhere, so maybe my past is catching up with me in ways I'm not aware of. And, look, maybe running a type of wine shanty is also in my future. This is a future I would not be opposed to.

Margaret eventually sold the pub and settled in the nearby Murray River town of Swan Hill, where she used the proceeds of the pub's sale to shore up a reasonably comfortable life for herself and her kids. An article unearthed by the show's researchers illustrates that her ex, who had spent most of their money, then tried to take everything Margaret had left. At a time in history when men were more likely to be believed, it's amazing that he was unsuccessful in his bid. When Margaret died she was written up in the local paper as an upstanding matriarch of the Swan Hill community.

So, in my family, two women, on either side, with little resources available to them, in a time when women were not allowed to take control, somehow, against the odds, took complete control of their lives under the worst of circumstances. They made good as best they could, despite the odds stacked against them.

For a woman like me, who never used to dwell in the past, someone who always looked ahead, there is a strength that comes from knowing that these women, their resilience, is in my blood. I can draw on this to give me perspective and solace when I need it, when I have to face difficult things of my own. There is something comforting in knowing I stand on the shoulders of all the women who have come before me, who survived and forged ahead, despite setbacks, to make things better.

Prior to filming this show I'd already committed to something that would become a huge new challenge for me and, not surprisingly, once I'd finished filming *Who Do You Think You Are?*, and learning about Maud and Margaret, I was even more committed to the cause.

During that long lockdown, shuffling around a big house with my pets, I realised it was time to follow through on something I'd always wanted to do but had never had the confidence to commit. I started foster care training. It was an intense course, and one I had no idea I would pass, but I eventually did.

I'd started the training long before I was asked to film the show. It's as if I was propelled by something outside of myself. Knowing that I could be there for kids in need (mostly in emergency placements, which would hopefully help to get them and their families back on their feet) is even more important now that I know that my own ancestor, Maud, never had access to that kind of care when she needed it desperately at seven years of age.

I consider myself lucky to meet these kids, who cope so incredibly well in extraordinarily tough situations, and while I have limited experience with kids I do hope I am providing a safe, warm and fun place to stay while their lives are upended for whatever reason. There are so many kids out there who need our help and it's the least I can do, for them, and for Maud, who I feel might be standing beside me to give me all the confidence I need to take on this next chapter in my life.

If I ever doubt myself, I will look back to Maud and Margaret and know I have what it takes. It's in my blood.

Private Dancer

(Mark Knopfler)

17.

Oh, the things I've learnt ...

For a woman who always said she didn't dwell on the past and preferred to look forward, I've realised the past can teach us a lot. Knowing what makes you feel good, what you would like to be better at, how strong you are, what you dream of, and how you can shore up your weaknesses and build on your strengths are all lessons the past teaches us. Age doesn't necessarily bring wisdom but it does bring acceptance and daring, or has for me, because I've let go of trying to twist myself to please others. And I've learnt other things too.

1. *It's best not to give a fuck.*
Thanks to the Museum of Old and New Art (MONA) in Tasmania, I was invited to discuss the representation of

women in art and music about seven years ago. I was going to be alongside a woman who wrote a book that completely changed how Western women saw themselves and their roles in society in the 1970s. The book was *The Female Eunuch* and the woman, Germaine Greer. Look, I know that Germaine has shared views of late that some consider a little on the nose but, back in the early days, she was a game changer and must have had skin as thick as the Sydney Harbour Bridge to be as brave as she was.

I met Germaine prior to sitting on the panel. She was, as I expected, pretty terrifying. And I'm a feminist.

When I asked Germaine if she was going to frock up for the occasion, the look on her face at the mere suggestion was everything. If I could have backed out, beeping like a truck, I would have.

And then later, as we sat on stage waiting for the audience to arrive, me, being a people-pleaser, asked Germaine, 'Are you okay sitting where you are?', thinking we could change seats if she wanted to move. She looked me dead in the eye and, without a hint of irony, she said, 'I DON'T GIVE A FUCK.' I nearly fell off my chair. She really didn't give one. Sure, I don't have a revolutionary feminist text behind me and PhDs coming out my woo ha to give me that kind of confidence, but I reckon caring less about the small things, about how people perceive us, what they might be saying about us, isn't such a bad thing. What I learnt from this experience was to simply get on with things and stop sweating the small stuff. Seems obvious now, really.

2. Sleeping tablets, champagne and long-haul flights don't mix.

Look, I'm not proud of this one, but take this as a lesson learnt, so you don't have to. When I was living in London I was flying back and forth to Australia for work quite regularly. I started to think that I was quite the seasoned traveller. The turnarounds between flying and working on arrival were small, so the aim was to try and sleep as much as possible on the plane to avoid the inevitable and horrible jet lag. This is where the sleeping tablets came in. I would take them to help. On one particular trip, I was upgraded to business class, which, of course, meant a cause for celebration. Any chance to lie horizontal on a long-haul flight deserves a party. Yes, I was absolutely going to drink all the French champagne if it was offered. And offered it was. This flight was like one of those bottomless brunches people buy on Groupon, where the food is ordinary but the mimosas flow, only it was French champagne and I was in for the long haul, literally.

When it was time to sleep, after many a champers, I popped a sleeping tablet, hoping for a blissful and long nap. I vaguely remember thinking the first tablet wasn't working. So I took another. It seems I continued to enjoy the champagne.

I have no idea how much champagne I had, and I don't remember much about the trip at all. I finally fell asleep, reclining like a queen. I thought I was in my business-class bed. It wasn't long before I fell off my throne.

In the morning, I was woken with a shake to be told that breakfast would be served. I was rapt. I love airline food. There's something about a highly processed meal in the air that reminds me of the pre-packaged TV dinners I'd seen on American TV shows as a kid, and I just can't say no. Ever. I inhaled my omelette, roasted tomato and mushrooms, a coffee, croissant and an orange juice (of course I ate everything on offer), none the wiser to what had gone down the night before. If you can't remember the party were you really partying?

After landing, it was time to stand up and grab my bag out of the overhead locker, a cacophony of feelings – hot, cold, nausea, sweats – washed over me. Could this be a hangover? The answer was definitively yes, and as I disembarked the plane in Bangkok via a very long, very hot passenger tube, I felt the full force of regret for what I had unknowingly done during the night. I was about to enjoy the full gamut of a raging hangover. When I finally exited the tunnel my eyes darted around desperately, searching for a bathroom, because I was feeling a little on the queasy side. All I could see was more passageways and travellators. There was no bathroom and nowhere to escape.

The final humiliation hit when I realised I had no other option but to search for the only bin available, which was the one full of headphones for passengers embarking on the next flight. As I held my own hair and heaved up the contents of my breakfast into the headphone bin, passengers continued to disembark behind me. Just as my body convulsed a teenager walked by and yelled, 'Love *Spicks and Specks*!' That wasn't the worst of it though. I was subsequently escorted to my next gate by fully armed Thai security guards with machine guns, possibly suspecting that I might be carrying drugs. The whole experience and the thought of spending a night in a Thai gaol had me seriously questioning my life choices. Fortunately, the guards dropped me at the airline lounge and I resolved never to combine sleeping pills and champagne again.

3. If you want to check out the Prime Minister's Office in Canberra, don't talk politics.

Every year the ABC rolls out some of their personalities and ships them to Canberra to spend one night at Parliament House, to chat with politicians at a little function. As the ABC relies on funding from the government, this is a PR exercise, of sorts. For those invited, it's a chance to stand on some of the plushest carpet in the land (seriously, it's like there's a mattress topper under the carpet, it's so bouncy) and to press the flesh with politicians of all persuasions.

The year I attended I was in the middle of making my doco *Nice* – about the things we grew up with that had a greater impact on us than we thought. The design episode was centred around the furniture and knick-knacks that featured in many a good room around the country, and not the classy stuff either. At the Canberra ABC showcase, I got talking to someone who was a fan of *Spicks and Specks*, a staffer for the then prime minister, Julia Gillard (who was also a fan, apparently). Parliament House is chock-full of Australian-designed furniture and art, and is a celebration of the highest quality work. As it should be.

After talking at length with the staffer about my show, I was invited to meet the prime minister and check out the furniture in her office. The staffer said the chairs were a peach colour, popular in the '80s, and a style that wouldn't be out of place in a design magazine now. They referred to them as 'the shit chairs', given they were thought to be quite dated (the '80s resurgence in furniture hadn't quite happened yet).

So, along the corridors we went, on a quest that not many Australians would have the opportunity to embark on, so I was feeling a bit chuffed. I stepped through the doorway of the office and there was our first female prime minister actually sitting in the '80s chairs! Ms Gillard warmly invited me in. I was a few champagnes down at this stage and keen for a natter, and the conversation was so jovial we took photos of us in those chairs and somehow I wrangled an opportunity to sit at the prime minister's desk. There I was, in the highest office in the country, pretending to lead the country, just for one second.

I'm still amazed this ever happened, given how the world and security has changed so much in the intervening years. I'd be lucky to be let into the café of Parliament House these days, let alone the PM's office. Just know that it felt good in that office, and I wouldn't mind spending more time in there ... especially with my shoes off enjoying that lush carpet.

4. Rich people don't have to dress up for parties.

One of the strangest (and therefore one of the best) gigs I've had was to be invited by Channel Ten to be the cultural attaché covering the Sochi Winter Olympics in Russia in 2014. I was asked to cover things like the very healthy underground drag scene, the protests around the games, and the creative arts scene in Sochi. At the time, Channel Ten was being run by two of Australia's biggest names, James Packer and Lachlan Murdoch. Towards the end of the Olympics, they hosted a party for select

Channel Ten folk in an amazing apartment atop of what I guess was the Russian Alps. It was, as you would expect, a very ritzy gathering. Beluga caviar was on offer and vodka was on tap (and if you think I didn't indulge in that, you're mistaken, because I wasn't sure I'd ever have the opportunity again!).

The night went swimmingly. I chatted to all and sundry and felt like I was truly living my best life. I must admit I was taken aback by the fact that, while we guests were all dressed up to the nines for this rare treat, our hosts had taken a rather more relaxed approach. This may be because they wanted to be considered men of the people, and I guess Lachlan Murdoch choosing to wear jeans isn't unusual, however, James Packer's choice of fleecy black tracksuit pants for the occasion left me confused. He was wearing *tracksuit pants*? Not snazzy fashion ones, but plain black fleecy ones that looked like they were from Kmart. It sure hinted at the fact that rich folk don't need to dress up to impress like the rest of us. And I guess if you're paying for the Beluga caviar, you don't need to prove anything.

During the party I saw James (a smoker) sucking on a dart or ten, so thought it might be a nice ice-breaker to ask one of the richest people in the world if I could have one too. I didn't smoke but, hell, everyone knows all the good chats happen in the smokers' area and I love a good story, so I thought, why not?

To be refused a cigarette by one of the richest men in the world was a thud back to earth that I wasn't expecting. 'It's me last one,' he said, and shuffled off as only a wealthy man in trackies can. Even though James Packer probably had people who could go and get him some more cigarettes, at any time of the day or night, I wasn't worth the last dart. Perhaps if *I* had been wearing tracksuit pants he might have changed his mind.

5. Say yes to a Russian banya.

While I was in Russia, I encountered the Russian version of a wellness treatment that will be permanently etched in my memory – the Russian banya (sauna). Our crew took a day off to enjoy this treat, not knowing entirely what to expect.

We were peeled off one by one for our turn in the mystical smoking banya shed. Wearing only bathers and a felt cloche-type hat in the shape of an acorn, which was tight and low on the face, we were individually ushered into a tin shed that was heated to an almost unbearable temperature. When it was my turn, I discovered two men inside, their hats pulled down like balaclavas so I could barely see their eyes, both of them naked from the waist up. What on earth was I in for? Sweating through fear and unbearable sauna-like heat, I had to lie on what seemed like a primitive operating table, while the men proceeded to pour freezing cold water on my hatted head to cool my face down, and then hit me with a bunch of twigs (they're actually birch tree branches that are apparently good for the skin) over and over again. It was a steam clean with added slaps of epic proportions.

Then, at what seemed to be the end of the slapping, the men proceeded to grab towels and whip them into the air like helicopter propellors. At this point I was so deliriously hot and confused I'd completely given over to the experience, or gone into freeze mode. I was ushered outside into the snow, where a bucket of ice-cold water was poured over me, before being instructed to get into what was a huge cauldron to slowly boil away over an open fire, my pink skin practically ready to peel off for eating. The final part of the process had me resting, like meat at the end of cooking, lying on a long swing outside, wrapped head to toe in woollen blankets. If someone had popped an apple in my mouth at that point I would have understood why. Worth it though.

6. *Everyone looks the same when naked en masse.*
I bared all for art, once, way back in 2001, when photographer Spencer Tunick decided to photograph Melburnians, nude, on the Princes Bridge. It was a freezing cold, rainy day and we had a 4 am start to be there for the sunrise, but, like 5000 other Melburnians,

I felt it was my duty to be a part of something quite phenomenal and show my support for the arts. We wanted Victoria to have the best turnout in the world for Tunick's naked photoshoot. I was also pretty young and wanted to embrace nudity without shame. It was an invigorating experience that I don't regret ... mostly.

Like I said, it was a very early wake-up call and I hadn't done my hair or put on any makeup, knowing it wouldn't matter given I'd be in a sea of people. When Tunick yelled through a megaphone, 'Okay, everybody, take your clothes off now,' I stripped off right next to the Arts Centre where I'd only ever gone fully clothed. It was oddly terrifying. Especially if someone decided to steal your knickers or your car keys while you were gone. Having no pockets in our nude suits meant we weren't allowed to hold on to anything as it would spoil the overall aesthetic. As we walked towards the position on the bridge, the feeling was one of euphoria, regardless of the frostbite that was clearly setting in on some folks' nether regions (I've never heard so many fellas apologising for the fact that it was SO cold). I got to see what we looked like as a group. And, frankly, we're all perfectly lovely as we are, and strangely, regardless of weight or body type, when we're all together, we all look the same. It was liberating. I felt empowered by this knowledge, and it helped with my body confidence for years to come.

What didn't help was the fact that a friend's brother was reading a men's magazine, *Dingo Magazine* (remember those mags, full of not-quite porn for men that were so popular in the '90s and 2000s?), a little while later. He came across a page of pics from the nude shoot under the heading, 'Cor, tits in Melbourne'. Of course, front and centre was me, arm-in-arm with my girlfriends, walking along without a care in the world.

Sending nudes wasn't as commonplace as it is now – we could only talk and text on our phones back then – so the idea of a nude photo out in the public was utterly mortifying to me. And the fact that I hadn't done my hair for the shoot ...

So I've walked nude on the streets of Melbourne *and* been in a men's magazine. I sound a helluva lot more adventurous than I really am. But I am glad I did it because, like Mark Twain says, you will be more disappointed by the things you didn't do than by the ones you did!

7. *Other women are not your enemy.*

Until the last fifty or so years, where women have gained more autonomy over their lives, society was structured in a way that meant women needed men for survival – financially that is. I know it's ridiculous to think that now, but truly, when you can't work and earn, you don't have any power. That previous dependency set us all up to mistrust anyone who could threaten our self-sufficiency. In work environments that are still mostly dominated by men, there is a scarcity of jobs for women, so we end up competing for those one or two seats at the table and it's natural to see other women as competition.

One of the greatest lessons I've learnt is to unlearn those kinds of deeply ingrained thoughts. Women can be your best allies.

Not that you're supposed to like all other women, that's simply not possible. But when I decided to flip this narrative and see other women as allies rather than potential threats, I've had some of the best working and creative relationships in my career. Working with Zan Rowe on *Bang On* has been a delight, and our collective creativity is undeniably more powerful together than apart, and our friendship runs deep. So leave that enemy stuff behind.

8. Some things will come full circle in the best possible ways.

Picture this. I'm in primary school. I've decided that I'm going to do a performance for the class. I'm not sure if this was requested or if I foisted it on everyone without asking if they were interested. That, or it was one of those rainy days when the teacher either rolls in the one television and video tape on a trolley to watch a nature doco or asks the kids to put on a show, because they need a laugh to ward off a crippling hangover. Anyways, there I was, doing a dance in front of the class to my favourite song, Tina Turner's 'Private Dancer', a song about a dancer who dances for money in a club, a woman who did whatever they wanted her to do. I danced with a walking stick so I could move around tap-dance style and, of course, a chair, to pull all the exotic dancer's moves on. *I was in grade four.* Luckily, I was oblivious to the true meaning of the song. I just loved Tina so much.

Pretty sure I gave the teacher a huge laugh that day ...

Years later, Mike Chapman, the Australian songwriter and producer who was responsible for some of the greatest hits of all time (and I mean this literally, such as Toni Basil's 'Mickey' and Pat Benatar's 'Love is a Battlefield') and who produced records like Blondie's breakthrough *Parallel Lines* and The Knack's record that featured 'My Sharona', was a guest on *Spicks and Specks*. It was an honour to meet such a legend. We often went out for a drink after taping the shows and after this show Mike came along.

He was a delightful gent who had stories for days. I loved talking to him.

We got along so well he offered me, and my then partner, the chance to go and stay at his holiday apartment in Noosa, which he himself rarely got to visit. *Why not?*

I thought. Noosa's a gorgeous part of the world and I'd look good living my best life for a few days in a penthouse suite.

So I took up Mike's offer and arrived at the impressive apartment. When I pressed the doorbell, it was not the usual *ding dong*, it was a recording of another of Mike's hits: '(Simply) The Best', sung by Tina Turner. I've never wanted a doorbell more. And, yes, it's probably the closest I'll ever get to this absolute legend of a woman who survived against all odds (after escaping a violent marriage to Ike and losing all of her money she then managed to resurrect her career while in her forties, and become one of the world's biggest pop stars). She is an absolute queen.

But it is sad that she'll never get to see my dance routine (I still remember all the moves!) of 'Private Dancer'.

9. *Always sing duets at karaoke.*

This is a no-brainer. Everyone knows that karaoke is fun for the first line or two of a song but then the realisation that you're stuck up there and have to keep singing for the next three or four minutes is akin to torture. Especially if you're bombing or people lose interest. So, my remedy is always choose a duet, because then at least you're not alone. 'Islands in the Stream' is my go-to for obvious reasons, but you're welcome to it if you ever are in need of inspiration.

10. *When you think that you are too old for something new, ignore your inner critic and just do it!*

I was the ripe old age of thirty-nine when I decided to up sticks and give London a go, thinking I could start a new life somewhere else with little but my reputation and a few *Spicks and Specks* DVDs to hand out. It was a luxury to be able to do this – for friends with kids it was unimaginable. So I promised to make the most of it. Which I did. But it didn't really work out workwise. Starting from scratch in a business that relies on people knowing who you are was a big ask. While I didn't succeed in breaking in over there, I made lifelong friends and learnt a lot about myself outside of the spotlight.

While in London I supplemented my income with work from Channel Ten's current affairs program *The Project*. It was an absolute dream. Because London is far closer to New York and Paris than Australia, I was sent to what's known as press junkets, which is a day where the stars of a movie or television show, or a singer or band releasing a single or album, talk to every imaginable press outlet possible from all over the world in the shortest amount of time.

I interviewed some of the hugest names on the planet. I stayed in magnificent hotels in classy areas of town I could never afford and, for a moment, I would pretend that this was my real life, which I guess it was, for a day or two.

There are things I learnt from doing press junket interviews that I feel I should share.

You will line up like cattle outside a room where a celebrity will sit all day and do interview after interview after interview. Your name will get called, you will enter the room, and then get three to five minutes to connect. Best of luck.

The actor or musician is probably as bored as batshit and has said the same things all day and can't remember who they said them to and if they even said them at all. So remember:

- When you're flown to New York to interview AC/DC and Angus Young offers you a cigarette, YOU HAVE ONE. Even if you don't smoke. Don't say no because then there's no story.
- When you ask Sting if the rumours are true and that he engages in hours-long tantric sex with his wife and thinks the body is a self-cleaning vessel, which means he doesn't have to wash, he will say yes to one of these and I'm not telling you which.
- If you accidentally flash Justin Timberlake as you're climbing up to sit on one of the stupid tall director's chairs that are barstool height because you're only five foot nothing, he will be

decent enough to avert his eyes and then ask the camera person to raise the frame a little, so no one else has to see that you're wearing your big undies.

- In order to stave off boredom, Julia Roberts will start asking you questions about your name, your family and it will be super weird for the roles of journo and subject to be reversed, especially when it's done by the Pretty Woman herself.

- Matt Damon is nice and will take it very well when you wish him 'best of luck with everything' at the end of the interview. As if he needs luck.

- When asked if she was really okay because she was so busy, Beyoncé will almost drop her guard for a second and you'll feel like you truly connect for a moment (this was at the time of Jay-Z's rumoured cheating after their first child in the middle of a huge world tour, when any normal person would be a mess!). However, she pulled it together as only Queen Bey could, proving that we're not worthy of her exceptional professionalism. There's a reason she's the best.

- Idris Elba is as handsome and as charming as you would expect.

- Ashton Kutcher's role as Steve Jobs will be forgotten almost immediately, but it was worth a quick trip to Paris.
- You will wait for hours to interview Snoop Dogg in Spain and, yes, you will get a high from just being in the room with him and will love the fact that he said he appreciated your ample trunk (it was an animation about cars, so any kind of car boot talk was relevant!).
- You do not catch 'the fever' from touching Justin Bieber.
- You will spend an entire interview nervously rubbing what you thought was the coffee table leg with your foot during an interview with Keanu Reeves, only to find out at the end it was not the coffee table, but Keanu's leg. He is a very polite man.

11. *Being alone doesn't have to be lonely.*

After nearly two years of lockdown in Melbourne, most of it living on my own, I had no choice but to face myself, in the rawest of ways. Day after day it was me, myself and I, except for the times I could walk or exercise with a friend, who lived in my five-kilometre radius. It was an experience done willingly for the greater good, I was proud to help reduce the inevitable Covid spread among the vulnerable, but it was a time that really pushed me personally. All those years when I'd been so busy, filling my days with a million things, were gone. I was left to deal with whoever I was without all of that.

Around this time, when I was struggling a little with loneliness, I read an inspirational quote on Instagram (author unknown or, more likely, not paid attention to because I was scrolling feverishly to ward off the anxiety in my brain) that spoke to my current condition of being single, locked in and lonely.

It went a little something like this. No other person will complete the complicated jigsaw of your life. You need to complete that jigsaw for yourself. And if you are by yourself, being alone is not lonely, even though it feels like that sometimes. You are simply by yourself. You are *with* yourself. And once you realise that, things will get a whole lot easier. Hopefully this will give you room to make choices that might be a bit more suitable for you.

Something clicked and I started to see my alone time as a gift, and an opportunity to really get to know myself, and not some kind of failure.

Knowing all of this earlier might have made my younger years a little less difficult to navigate and taken the pressure off. Until then I thought I had to somehow get life 'right', partner up, etc.

So I've got some advice to tell younger me that I would probably never listen to given my high school report said, and I quote (I found it the other day): 'The bulk of the information Myfanwy lacks is born out of class discussion, where notes have to be taken, and you have to LISTEN to what's being said. At this stage Myfanwy is certainly lacking in the latter.'

But if younger me was open to listening, I'd tell her, life isn't a romance novel that ties up neatly at the end. We all saw the perfect example of that when even the handsome '80s Mills and Boon cover star, Fabio, got hit in his beautiful face by a bird while riding on a rollercoaster. #neverforget.

So I'd tell younger me this: keep loving with all of your big dumb heart and you will be okay. And remember to throw a bit of love and care to yourself sometimes, too. Because that's just as important. And you're pretty okay company just as you are.

Acknowledgements

My publisher told me that the acknowledgement section is like a speech at the Logies, but better, so given I'll probably never receive my own personal Logie I guess this is my moment. Buckle up, and this time I promise not to swear.

Thank you to my family, Ed, Nancye, Shaun, Andre and Kit and all your beautiful partners, Anne and Siobhann, and Bec and the kids. Without you I am nothing, literally.

To Vanessa, my publisher, for being absolutely delightful to work with through this whole process and for putting up with me routinely dragging my deadlines out close to the wire. Jacquie Brown who swooped in and worked on the final rushed edits, you're amazing. What a dream team that I'm blessed to have found during this process.

To Jacinta Waters, my original manager who brokered this book deal and whose support has got me through some of the best and the worst times of my life, some that I've written about in this book. You've held my hand and my secrets for years, so I'm looking forward to being able to offer the same to you now, as a friend.

To Helen and Olivia at Creative Representation and of course Kevin at Token who have helped me steer this thing to its final destination. In the words of Tina Turner, you're simply the best.

To Katrina Lamaro and Helen Walk, our weekly exercise sessions and friendship saved me in lockdown and continue to give me life to this day. So many hearty laughs were had when they were desperately needed, and your support spurred me on to keep writing, even when I didn't want to. I couldn't have survived the last few years without your love, humour and support.

To my wonderful girlfriends (in no particular order), Georgi Herrick, Beth Tobin, Kate Radford, Kirsty Bradmore, Samantha Clode, Susie Jones, Rachel Brown, Johanna Greenway, Lucinda Eastwood, Katia Zanutta, Alicia Brown, Stephanie Ashworth, Elise Barnfather, Nerida Leggat, Vicki Kerrigan, Kate McMillan, Nadine Cohen and Nina Agzarian. I'm the luckiest gal in the world to count you as friends. Without your endless support I wouldn't have believed I had a book in me. Thanks, too, for reminding me of things when I couldn't remember, which was often.

To Jess Keely, Ben Fletcher, SJ, Jo and Jess Lilley, who provided such support to me during my time living in London and beyond, especially for all the very early chats that went long into the night, which eventually led to this. You all know this book has been a long time coming.

Hayley Crane and Barb Heggin, the best radio producers in the land. I didn't write much about our time working together, but please know that a lot of this book wouldn't exist without your love and support.

To Michelle and Crickette, thanks for being so welcoming towards me, and easing me into this new stage of my life. You are the givers of local knowledge and local laughs and I am very grateful for your friendship.

Zan and my glorious Bang Fam who listen to our podcast. Zan, you've been such a huge part of my life over the last few years; it's meant the world to me, and I can't believe what a beautiful community we've created. Thank you.

To Mike's family, thank you for allowing me to write about your son and brother. Mike's love lives on in you all.

To Alan and Adam, I've got one word for you both ... BABE.

To Joel and Jack, the best travel buddies in the world, I adore you both.

To Brian for opening your home and your heart to me during this writing process. Thank you for your kindness and unwavering support and for putting up with me plonked on your kitchen table taking up space in your home in more ways than one.

hachette
AUSTRALIA

If you would like to find out more about
Hachette Australia, our authors, upcoming events
and new releases you can visit our website or our
social media channels:

hachette.com.au
HachetteAustralia
HachetteAus